The Gospel of Luke, often mined for information about the life of Jesus, is also one of the earlier Christian examples of narrative theology. Unlike some writers of New Testament books, Luke has engaged in the theological task by shaping a narrative representation of the coming and mission of Jesus. In doing so, he goes to great lengths to ground the work of Jesus in the continuing story of God's redemptive plan, especially witnessed in the Scriptures, and he also emphasizes the ongoing character of that story, with the result that Luke's audience is challenged to discern the purpose of God in order that they may embrace it and order their lives around it. This exploration of the way in which Luke accomplishes his theological task in the first century is both informative and illuminating for contemporary readers seeking approaches to cultural criticism and constructive theology today.

NEW TESTAMENT THEOLOGY

General Editor: James D. G. Dunn,
Lightfoot Professor of Divinity, University of Durham

The theology of the Gospel of Luke

This series provides a programmatic survey of the individual writings of the New Testament. It aims to remedy the deficiency of available published material, which has tended to concentrate on historical, textual, grammatical, and literary issues at the expense of the theology, or to lose distinctive emphases of individual writings in systematized studies of 'The Theology of Paul' and the like. New Testament specialists here write at greater length than is usually possible in the introductions to commentaries or as part of other New Testament theologies, and explore the theological themes and issues of their chosen books without being tied to a commentary format, or to a thematic structure drawn from elsewhere. When complete, the series will cover all the New Testament writings, and will thus provide an attractive, and timely, range of texts around which courses can be developed.

THE THEOLOGY OF THE GOSPEL OF LUKE

JOEL B. GREEN

Associate Professor of New Testament
American Baptist Seminary of the West and
Graduate Theological Union, Berkeley, California

CAMBRIDGE
UNIVERSITY PRESS

Published by the Press Syndicate of the University of Cambridge
The Pitt Building, Trumpington Street, Cambridge CB2 1RP
40 West 20th Street, New York, NY 10011–4211, USA
10 Stamford Road, Oakleigh, Melbourne 3166, Australia

First published 1995

Printed in Great Britain at the University Press, Cambridge

A catalogue record for this book is available from the British Library

Library of Congress cataloguing in publication data

Green, Joel B., 1956–
The theology of the gospel of Luke / Joel B. Green.
p.   cm. – (New Testament theology)
Includes bibliographical references and indexes.
ISBN 0 521 46529 x (hardback) – ISBN 0 521 46932 5 (paperback)
1. Bible. N.T. Luke – Criticism, interpretation, etc. 1. Title.
II. Series.
BS2595.2.G74 1995
226.4′06 – dc20   94–28658   CIP

ISBN 0 521 46529 x hardback
ISBN 0 521 46932 5 paperback

Contents

Editor's preface

Although the New Testament is usually taught within Departments or Schools or Faculties of Theology/Divinity/Religion, theological study of the individual New Testament writings is often minimal or at best patchy. The reasons for this are not hard to discern.

For one thing, the traditional style of studying a New Testament document is by means of straight exegesis, often verse by verse. Theological concerns jostle with interesting historical, textual, grammatical and literary issues, often at the cost of the theological. Such exegesis is usually very time-consuming, so that only one or two key writings can be treated in any depth within a crowded three-year syllabus.

For another, there is a marked lack of suitable textbooks round which courses could be developed. Commentaries are likely to lose theological comment within a mass of other detail in the same way as exegetical lectures. The section on the theology of a document in the Introduction to a commentary is often very brief and may do little more than pick out elements within the writing under a sequence of headings drawn from systematic theology. Excursuses usually deal with only one or two selected topics. Likewise larger works on New Testament Theology usually treat Paul's letters as a whole and, having devoted the great bulk of their space to Jesus, Paul, and John, can spare only a few pages for others.

In consequence, there is little incentive on the part of teacher or student to engage with a particular New Testament document, and students have to be content with a general overview, at best complemented by in-depth study of (parts of)

two or three New Testament writings. A serious corollary to
this is the degree to which students are thereby incapacitated
in the task of integrating their New Testament study with the
rest of their Theology or Religion courses, since often they are
capable only of drawing on the general overview or on a
sequence of particular verses treated atomistically. The
growing importance of a literary-critical approach to individual documents simply highlights the present deficiencies
even more. Having been given little experience in handling
individual New Testament writings as such at a theological
level, most students are very ill-prepared to develop a properly
integrated literary and theological response to particular texts.
Ordinands too need more help than they currently receive
from textbooks, so that their preaching from particular passages may be better informed theologically.

There is need therefore for a series to bridge the gap between
too brief an introduction and too full a commentary where
theological discussion is lost among too many other concerns.
It is our aim to provide such a series. That is, a series where
New Testament specialists are able to write at a greater length
on the theology of individual writings than is usually possible
in the introductions to commentaries or as part of New Testament Theologies, and to explore the theological themes and
issues of these writings without being tied to a commentary
format or to a thematic structure provided from elsewhere. The
volumes seek both to describe each document's theology, and
to engage theologically with it, noting also its canonical
context and any specific influence it may have had on the
history of Christian faith and life. They are directed at those
who already have one or two years of full-time New Testament
and theological study behind them.

University of Durham   JAMES D. G. DUNN

Preface

It will surprise many readers to discover that Luke is responsible for more material, measured in sheer words, than any other New Testament writer. This is surprising because his influence as a theologian has not often been felt in such explicit ways when compared with Paul or John. Indeed, it is only in recent decades that the expression "Luke *the theologian*" has become a commonplace, and it is personally satisfying to be able to participate in this way in the recovery of Lukan theology for the church.

My own appreciation for Luke has developed in conversation with my students, former and present – first at New College Berkeley, and now at the American Baptist Seminary of the West and Graduate Theological Union, Berkeley. In particular, I have benefited from interactions with Meagan Howland and Michael McKeever, both of whom have served in varying capacities as research assistants and conversation partners. I am grateful to them; to the Graduate Theological Union, who awarded Michael and me a Henry Mayo Newhall Fellowship for Student–Faculty Partnership for work on "Luke–Acts and the Jewish People"; and to the Catholic Biblical Association, who awarded me a Young Scholar's Fellowship for work on the application of discourse theory to the Gospel of Luke. I am also indebted to the Friday Night Fellowship of St. Luke's United Methodist Church, Richmond, California; together we have been working through the Gospel of Luke and its implications for faithful discipleship for almost two years – with no end yet in sight!

xi

Abbreviations

AB	Anchor Bible
ABD	*The Anchor Bible Dictionary.* 6 vols. Edited by David Noel Freedman. New York: Doubleday, 1992.
AMTBBB	Athenäum^s Monografien: Theologie; Bonner Biblische Beiträge
AnBib	Analecta Biblica
ANRW	*Aufstieg und Niedergang der Römischen Welt: Geschichte und Kultur Roms im Spiegel der Neueren Forschung.* Edited by Hildegard Temporini. Berlin: Walter de Gruyter.
AS	Advances in Semiotics
AUS	American University Studies
BBR	*Bulletin of Biblical Research*
BETL	Bibliotheca ephemeridum theologicarum lovaniensium
Bib	*Biblica*
BJS	Brown Judaic Studies
ConBNT	Coniectanea biblica, New Testament
CBQ	*Catholic Biblical Quarterly*
CTL	Cambridge Textbooks in Linguistics
DJG	*Dictionary of Jesus and the Gospels.* Edited by Joel B. Green and Scot McKnight. Downers Grove, Illinois; Leicester: Inter-Varsity, 1992
EDNT	*Exegetical Dictionary of the New Testament.* 3 vols. Edited by Horst Balz and Gerhard Schneider. Grand Rapids, Michigan: Wm.B. Eerdmans, 1990–93

EKKNT	Evangelisch-Katholischer Kommentar zum Neuen Testament
FB	Forschung zur Bibel
FF	Foundations and Facets
FRLANT	Forschungen zur Religion und Literatur des Alten und Neuen Testaments
GP	Gospel Perspectives
HCPE	Health Care Policy and Ethics
IBRB	Institute for Biblical Research Bibliography
IDB	*The Interpreter's Dictionary of the Bible*. 4 vols. Edited by George Arthur Buttrick. Nashville: Abingdon, 1962
ISBL	Indiana Studies in Biblical Literature
JBL	*Journal of Biblical Literature*
JSNT	*Journal for the Study of the New Testament*
JSNTSS	Journal for the Study of the New Testament Supplement Series
JSOTSS	Journal for the Study of the Old Testament Supplement Series
LCBI	Literary Currents in Biblical Interpretation
LEC	Library of Early Christianity
LS	Language in Society
NICNT	New International Commentary on the New Testament
NIDNTT	*The New International Dictionary of New Testament Theology*. 3 vols. Edited by Colin Brown. Grand Rapids, Michigan: Zondervan, 1975–78.
NIGTC	New International Greek Testament Commentary
NIV	New International Version
NovT	*Novum Testamentum*
NRSV	New Revised Standard Version
NTS	*New Testament Studies*
OBT	Overtures to Biblical Theology
OTKNT	Okumenischer Taschenbuch-kommentar zum Neuen Testament
PRCS	Parallax Re-visions of Culture and Society
PTMS	Princeton Theological Monograph Series

RB	*Revue Biblique*
RST	Regensburger Studien zur Theologie
SANT	Studien zum Alten und Neuen Testament
SBLDS	Society of Biblical Literature Dissertation Series
SBLMS	Society of Biblical Literature Monograph Series
SCL	Sather Classical Lectures
SHM	Studies in the History of Missions
SNTSMS	Society of New Testament Studies Monograph Series
SNTU	Studien zum Neuen Testament und seiner Umwelt
SNTW	Studies of the New Testament and Its World
SP	Sacra Pagina
SS	Studies in Scripture
SSG	Studies in the Synoptic Gospels
TDNT	*Theological Dictionary of the New Testament.* 10 vols. Edited by Gerhard Kittel and Gerhard Friedrich. Grand Rapids, Michigan: Wm. B. Eerdmans, 1964–76.
TEV	Today's English Version
TI	Theological Inquiries
TPINTC	Trinity Press International New Testament Commentary
TR	Theology and Religion
TynB	*Tyndale Bulletin*
UBS³	*The Greek New Testament.* 3rd ed. Edited by Kurt Aland, *et al.* London: United Bible Societies, 1975
WBC	Word Biblical Commentary
WS	Walberberger Studien
WSPL	Warwick Studies in Philosophy and Language
WUNT	Wissenschaftliche Untersuchungen zum Neuen Testament
WW	*Word and World*
ZNW	*Zeitschrift für die neutestamentliche Wissenschaft*
ZSNT	Zacchaeus Studies: New Testament

CHAPTER I

"In the days of King Herod of Judea": the world of Luke's Gospel

Of the Song of Mary (Luke 1:46–55) the poet Thomas John Carlisle writes,

> At our eternal peril
> we choose to ignore
> the thunder and the tenor
> of her song,
> its revolutionary beat.[1]

In doing so, Carlisle, perhaps paradoxically, brings to the foreground a distressing enigma. At least in this century readers of the Gospel of Luke *have* ignored "the thunder and tenor of her song." Or rather, more often than not, we have wrapped it in antiseptic dress, spiritualized it, projected its message of redemption-by-social-transformation into the eschaton.[2] More often than not, the Song of Mary has been the focus of tradition-historical investigation: who first wrote it? From what community did it derive? In what form did it come to Luke? Mary's Song has not often been read as integral to the narrative of Luke's Gospel, as integral to Luke's narrative theology, as deriving its meaning in *this* narrative co-text[3] and

---

[1] Thomas John Carlisle, "Revolutionary Carol," in *Beginning with Mary: Women of the Gospels in Portrait* (Grand Rapids, Michigan: Wm. B. Eerdmans, 1986) 4.

[2] See David M. Scholer, "The Magnificat (Luke 1:46–55): Reflections on Its Hermeneutical History," in *Conflict and Context: Hermeneutics in the Americas*, ed. Mark Lau Branson and C. René Padilla (Grand Rapids, Michigan: Wm. B. Eerdmans, 1986) 210–19.

[3] By "co-text" we mean the sentences and larger textual units surrounding the text and relating to it so as to constrain its interpretation. "Context" refers to the socio-historical setting of the text. See Gillian Brown and George Yule, *Discourse Analysis*, CTL (Cambridge University Press, 1983) 46–50.

thus from the larger theological program of the Third Evangelist. The same may be said of numerous other texts unique to Luke's Gospel: the Parable of the Good Samaritan, the Parable of the Prodigal Son, Jesus' words of forgiveness from the cross, and so on.

The study of the Song of Mary in this century is a paradigm of the study of the Third Gospel more generally. Only since World War II has the prospect of Luke as *theologian* begun to be taken with seriousness. Redaction criticism, which examined Luke's deployment of his presumed sources,[4] highlighted the possibility of a Lukan theological agenda, but did not yet embrace the potential of reading Luke's narrative *as a whole* as a theological document. Although Luke's combined work, Luke and Acts, contributes some 28 percent of the total volume of the New Testament (compared with 24 percent in the case of Paul),[5] he has not normally been listed alongside Jesus, Paul, and John in studies of New Testament theology.

Wider currents in theological and literary studies have begun to rectify this deficiency. Specifically, greater recognition of the embeddedness of all thought in tradition and story has opened up the potential for reading the Gospel of Luke, along with other narrative texts in Scripture, in fresh ways. If Lukan theology is embedded in narrative, however, that narrative is itself embedded in the world of the first-century Greco-Roman Mediterranean.

THE ''WORLDS'' OF LUKE

Despite its very different look, the Gospel of Luke shares a key similarity with the letters of Paul. Like them it is an *occasional* text. This encourages a reading of the Gospel that is sensitive, first, to the socio-historical circumstances within which the

---

[4] See especially Hans Conzelmann, *The Theology of St. Luke* (London: Faber and Faber, 1960); and the later response to Conzelmann, I. Howard Marshall, *Luke: Historian and Theologian* (Exeter: Paternoster; Grand Rapids, Michigan: Zondervan, 1970; 2nd ed., 1989).

[5] Words in the New Testament (UBS³): 137,888; in Luke–Acts: 37,951; in the wider Pauline corpus (13 letters): 32,429.

Gospel is set; and, second, to the more specific discourse situation giving rise to the narrative itself. The first concerns the world of the Gospel of Luke. The second is interested in exploring the purposeful communication of author and audience. Unlike Paul's letters, whose mode of argumentation has a more recognizably didactic and persuasive look, the Third Gospel presents its message in the form of a narrative. Its mode of persuasion is perhaps more subtle, but no less theological. In order to explore it a venture into its world is a necessity.

Indeed, in narrating his story Luke[6] employs cultural and chronological markers that manifestly root the Gospel in the late first century BCE and first third of the first century CE:

"In the days of King Herod of Judea..." (1:5),

"In those days a decree went out from Emperor Augustus ..." (2:1), and

"In the fifteenth year of the reign of Emperor Tiberius, when Pontius Pilate was governor of Judea ..." (3:1).

These geo-political markers, occurring in the early chapters of the Gospel, are some of the most obvious, but there are many others.

Some are quite subtle, including those that assume the cultural knowledge of an "insider." For example, the preface of Luke (1:1–4) situates the author socially as one capable of writing learned Greek, who may have trafficked in technical or professional writing, and who generally had an appreciation for the labors of those who work with their hands.[7] Again, the

---

[6] Like the other Gospels in the New Testament, the Gospel of Luke is the work of an anonymous writer. Traditionally, Luke, the sometime companion of Paul, has been identified as the author of the Gospel (cf. the "we sections" in Acts 16:10–17; 20:5–15; 21:1–18; 27:1–28:16; also Philem. 24; Col. 4:14). However, it is not clear that anything is gained for our reading of its *theology* by an unequivocal identification of its author. See the recent discussion of authorship in Joseph A. Fitzmyer, *Luke the Theologian: Aspects of His Teaching* (New York/Mahwah: Paulist, 1989) 1–26. Discussions of the Gospel have traditionally referred to "Luke" as the voice through which the story of Jesus' mission and message has been related, drawing attention to Luke in a role that closely approximates contemporary understanding of the "narrator." It is in this sense that "Luke" is used here. It is likewise difficult to determine with precision *when* the Gospel was written, though the most popular view is that it was written in the seventies or eighties CE.

[7] So Loveday C. A. Alexander, *The Preface to Luke's Gospel: Literary Convention and Social Context in Luke 1.1–4 and Acts 1.1*, SNTSMS 78 (Cambridge University Press, 1993);

opening of the narrative itself, in 1:5–7, posits a cultural enigma, claiming for Elizabeth and Zechariah a level of right-eousness before God that stands in serious tension with "what everybody knows." What everyone knows, or knew in the Judean world of antiquity, is that childlessness is a consequence of a blameworthy life and so a sign of God's curse.[8] Such examples are easily multiplied.

Some are difficult to decipher. (Why did Elizabeth remain in seclusion for five months following her conception? [1:24]) Others present more far-reaching, historical problems. (What are we to make of Luke's alleged census under Augustus? [2:1]) However troublesome these cultural and geo-political markers might have become for subsequent readings of Luke, they nevertheless demonstrate the degree to which this Gospel is rooted in a time and place. Luke's *narrative*, then, presents a *theological program* deeply embedded in the cultural currents of the first-century Mediterranean world.

More fundamentally of course, all language is embedded in culture,[9] and Luke's narrative provides no exception. In our reading of Luke's theology in the world of Luke, however, we must grapple with this axiom at three levels. There is, first, the "world of Luke's Gospel" understood in the sense noted above – that is, the world Luke's Gospel assumes, the world his Gospel claims to represent. It must be admitted, though, that Luke's account cannot capture the many and diverse ingre-dients of the real world of first-century Palestine. Hence, there is, second, the world *actualized* by Luke's narrative – that is, the world as Luke portrays it.[10] For example, we know that the temple in Jerusalem had asserted itself as a major economic and political force within Second Temple Judaism and thus

Alexander, "Luke's Preface in the Context of Greek Preface-Writing," *NovT* 28 (1986) 48–74.

8 Cf. Gen. 16:4; 29:32; 30:1, 22–23; 1 Sam. 1:5–6; Pss. 127:3–5; 128; Phyllis Trible, *God and the Rhetoric of Sexuality*, OBT (Philadelphia: Fortress, 1978) 34–38.

9 Michael Stubbs, *Discourse Analysis: The Sociolinguistic Analysis of Natural Language*, LS 4 (University of Chicago Press; Oxford: Basil Blackwell, 1983) 1–14.

10 For this notion of actualized as distinct from virtual properties, I have borrowed from the discussion of the basic semantic properties of sememes in Umberto Eco, *The Role of the Reader: Explorations in the Semiotics of Texts*, AS (Bloomington: Indiana University Press, 1979) 18.

throughout the "land of the Jews" with which Luke's Gospel is concerned. On the other hand, Luke's presentation of the temple almost completely sidesteps this historical reality. Instead, Luke *actualizes* other important aspects of the place of the temple in the life of the Jewish people. He portrays the temple as the locus of God's presence, a place of prayer, and an institution that served to perpetuate distinctions between Jews and non-Jews, priests and non-priests, men and women, and so on.

Third, "the world of Luke" signifies the world as Luke wants it to be, the world which, according to his theological perspective, God purposes. Thus, Luke is not content to present the world "as it really is," but purposefully shapes the story in such a way that some of its facets are undermined, others legitimated. To return to our earlier example, although it is a truism that the Jerusalem temple functioned as a vital economic center in the world of Jesus, Luke has very little to say on this matter. This is because, on the one hand, the economic issues Luke wants to address are far bigger than the temple; in fact, as we shall see, questions of economic exchange and economic power were integral to the Mediterranean world of which Jerusalem was a part; these Luke will work to undermine in his account, but not by a broadside against the temple.

On the other hand, Luke does not elaborate on the politico-economic power of the temple because for him the primary importance of the temple rests elsewhere, on its role as a "cultural center" (to use Clifford Geertz's terminology). Cultural centers are the active centers of social order: "essentially concentrated loci of serious acts, they consist in the point or points in a society where its leading ideas come together with its leading institutions to create an arena in which the events that most vitally affect its members' lives take place." They "mark the center [of the social world] as center and give what goes on there its aura of being not merely important but in some odd fashion connected with the way the world is built."[11]

---

[11] Clifford Geertz, "Centers, Kings, and Charism: Reflections on the Symbolics of Power," in *Local Knowledge: Further Essays in Interpretive Anthropology* (New York:

Luke's narrative undermines this key role of the temple first by
acknowledging it, and then by means of a slowly evolving,
increasingly negative characterization of the temple, trans-
forming the initially positive conception of the temple in Luke
1–2. In the Third Gospel, finally, at Jesus' death, Luke narrates in proleptic fashion the eventual and thoroughgoing
theological critique of the temple to follow in Acts 7.[12] So,
although it is helpful to know as much as we can about Luke's
world (in the first sense), it is just as critical if not even more so
to see how that world fares at the hands of the Evangelist *in the
world of the narrative itself*.

If we are concerned with the world of Luke, then, we must
attend to how his narrative *represents* and *challenges* the world
of the first-century Mediterranean. Consequently, we will be
interested above all in reading the Third Gospel on its own
terms, albeit against the backdrop of what we otherwise know
about the first-century world it purports to portray. The text
is thus given a chance, as it were, to speak back to, and
within, its own world. At the same time, in grappling with
how Luke embraces and critiques the commonly held views
and respected cultural institutions of his day, we may well
find our own conventional wisdom brought under suspicion,
our own prior understandings and pet convictions
assailed.[13]

Basic, 1983) 121–46 (122–23, 124). Cf. the very similar comments in Mary Douglas,
How Institutions Think, the Frank W. Abrams Lectures (Syracuse, New York:
Syracuse University, 1986).

[12] See Joel B. Green, "The Demise of the Temple as 'Culture Center' in Luke–Acts:
An Exploration of the Rending of the Temple Veil (Luke 23.44–49)," *RB*, forthcoming.

[13] Cf. Umberto Eco, *Semiotics and the Philosophy of Language*, AS (Bloomington:
Indiana University Press, 1984) 25: "A text is not simply a communicational
apparatus. It is a device which questions the previous signifying systems, often
renews them, and sometimes destroys them." On the importance of allowing social
analysis to bring into question one's own world view – an issue often neglected by
those who have seconded social analysis into New Testament studies – cf. George
E. Marcus and Michael M. J. Fischer, *Anthropology as Cultural Critique: An Experi-
mental Moment in the Human Sciences* (Chicago/London: University of Chicago Press,
1986).

LUKE'S JESUS IN CULTURAL CONTEXT

What are the key features of the cultural context of Luke's story of Jesus?[14] In subsequent chapters we will outline in more detail some of the following as it bears directly on our under-standing of the socio-historical realities within and to which Luke is addressing the "good news." Here, though, we may begin to describe the mural of Luke's world painted large.

First, from the opening verse of the Gospel, we are aware that Luke is concerned with *the political world* and *the balance of power* in Greco-Roman Palestine.[15] In fact, Luke's opening phrase, "in the days of King Herod of Judea" (1:5a), is far more than a vague chronological marker. Instead, it serves to draw attention to the social setting of these events in a par-ticular period of political tension. Herod came to power despite strong anti-Idumean feelings and, in particular, resistance to him among the Jewish elders in Jerusalem. His power base was purely secular, with no claim to God having chosen him for service as king of the Jews. This, together with problematic economic and cultural affairs associated with his reign, must be factored into any reading of "the days of King Herod." That these realities would not have been far from the minds of the narrator and his Greco-Roman audience is suggested not only by the notoriety of Herod's ignominious reign, but also by the pervasiveness of socio-political concerns throughout Luke 1–2.

The same can be said, for example, of the census, mentioned four times in the space of five verses (2:1–5). The prosperity and peace for which the Roman Empire is now known was

---

[14] See Henry J. Cadbury, *The Book of Acts in History* (New York: Harper, 1955); Marion L. Soards, "The Historical and Cultural Setting of Luke–Acts," in *New Views on Luke and Acts*, ed. Earl Richard (Collegeville, Minnesota: Liturgical, 1990) 33–47; Jerome H. Neyrey, ed., *The Social World of Luke–Acts: Models for Interpretation* (Peabody, Massachusetts: Hendrickson, 1991); Bruce J. Malina and Richard L. Rohrbaugh, *Social-Science Commentary on the Synoptic Gospels* (Minneapolis: Fortress, 1992) 279–413.

[15] See the sometimes extravagant claims on socio-political affairs in Luke 1–2 in J. Massyngbaerde Ford, *My Enemy Is My Guest: Jesus and Violence in Luke* (Maryknoll, New York: Orbis, 1984) 1–36; Richard A. Horsley, *The Liberation of Christmas: The Infancy Narratives in Social Context* (New York: Crossroad, 1989) 23–52.

produced through initial conquest and plunder, and maintained through subsequent taxation of a conquered people. And a census such as that named by Luke had as its purpose the·preparation of tax rolls. Moreover, the explicit naming of Emperor Augustus in 2:1 is of interest, for this refers to Octavian, who had been recognized as "the divine savior who has brought peace to the world."[16] That in this very context Jesus is presented as Savior, Lord, the one through whom peace comes to the world (2:11, 14), can hardly be accidental.

Furthermore, Mary's son, she is told, will have an everlasting kingdom, the throne of David (1:32–33). The Song of Mary portrays God's mighty acts of salvation as socio-political reversal, with the powerful brought down from their thrones and the lowly uplifted (1:52). The Song of Zechariah employs images of exodus while prophesying how "we would be saved from our enemies" (1:71; cf. 1:73). Simeon and Anna, in their respective hopes for "the consolation of Israel" and "redemption of Jerusalem," must also have in mind the cessation of foreign occupancy and subjection, the renewal of Israel as a nation under Yahweh (and not under the Roman emperor).

Luke thus makes his audience aware at the very outset that the narrative of "the events that have been fulfilled among us" (1:1) is set squarely in the midst of the political turmoil of the Roman occupation of Palestine. Other data underscore the importance of this aspect of Luke's world. The presence of a centurion in Capernaum is recorded in a matter-of-fact way (7:1–10) as is the execution of Galileans by Pilate (13:1–2). Within the Gospel narrative, Jesus himself predicts the destruction of Jerusalem by opposing armies (e.g., 21:20–24) – an event that, presumably, would have been remembered in the past by many of Luke's audience. That the Gospel of Luke moves forward to a *Roman* act of execution, the crucifixion of Jesus as a pretender to the throne (see esp. 23:2–5, 38), urges us to refuse any suggestion that the Roman political world is a mere "backdrop" to Luke's narrative.

Secondly, the social world which Luke represents is one in

16 Horsley, *Liberation*, 28.

which *eschatological anticipation* is rampant. If we recall that eschatological hope in its myriad forms focused preeminently on the coming of God to rule in peace and justice,[17] then we may also remind ourselves that eschatological hope within the Lukan narrative must be read against a socio-political backdrop. This is true inasmuch as the coming of God would bring an end to political dominance and social oppression. The appearance of Gabriel in Luke 1 indicates already the eschatologically charged atmosphere in which the birth narrative is set, for he is known to us in part as an interpreter of end-time visions (Dan. 8:16–26; 9:21–27). The association of John with the figure of Elijah, particularly against the backdrop of Mal. 3:1–2; 4:5–6 (cf. Luke 1:16–17, 76), continues this motif, as does the regularity with which the Holy Spirit appears in Luke's Infancy Gospel. The litany of references to the Spirit brings to mind the old prophecies about the eschatological coming of the Spirit (1:15, 35, 41, 67; 2:25, 26, 27; cf., e.g., Isa. 44:3–5; Ezek. 26:24–32; Joel 2:28–32). Differences of viewpoint about the sort of Messiah anticipated (and questions about how widespread in antiquity such expectation might have been) aside, the birth narrative repeatedly speaks of the coming of the Christ, and this advances even further the sense of eschatological anticipation in the narrative. Moreover, the eschatological visitation of God is noted in Luke 1:68; 2:38, signifying the appearance of divine help and deliverance. Finally, Mary, Zechariah, Simeon, and Anna each give expression to an expectation of God's end-time deliverance.[18] In these ways, the world into which Jesus was born in Luke is shown to be rife with eschatological anticipation – an anticipation with clear ramifications for the cessation of Israel's subjection to its Herodian and Roman overlords.

Third, it is immediately clear in the Third Gospel that the narrative to unfold will be concerned with issues of *social status and social stratification*. This is not to say that Luke is especially

---

[17] See, e.g., George R. Beasley-Murray, *Jesus and the Kingdom of God* (Grand Rapids, Michigan: Wm. B. Eerdmans, 1986) 3–68.

[18] See J. Bradley Chance, *Jerusalem, the Temple, and the New Age in Luke–Acts* (Macon, Georgia: Mercer University Press, 1988) 48–56.

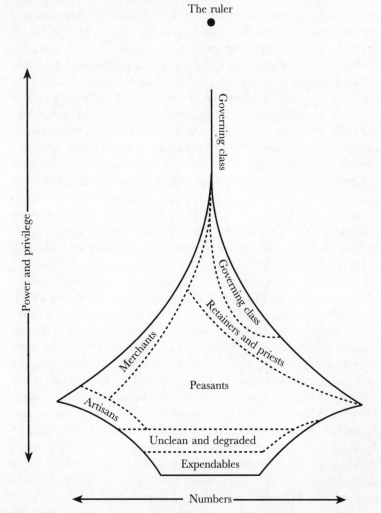

Figure 1   A graphic representation of the relationship among classes in
agrarian societies (from Gerhard Lenski, *Power and Privilege: A Theory of Social
Stratification*, 2nd ed. [Chapel Hill: University of North Carolina, 1984] 284).

concerned with economic class – for example, as a function of one's relative income or standard of living, or as connected to one's relationship with the means of production (as in Marxism). Such matters of industrial and post-industrial society have little meaning in Greco-Roman antiquity.[19] Rather, Luke's social world was defined around power and privilege (see figure 1), and is measured by a complex of phenomena – religious purity, family heritage, landownership (for non-priests), vocation, ethnicity, gender, education, and age.

Introduced with titles appropriate to their status are *King* Herod and *Emperor* Augustus (1:5; 2:1) – the former of whom would have had direct control over the whole region in which these events are located, the latter indirect. Their location on the diagram of social status is obvious. At the opposite end of these well-placed, powerful landowners on the social spectrum are the shepherds of 2:8–20, representative of the peasantry. Luke will introduce us to "unclean and degraded" persons and even an "expendable" (see Luke 16:20–21) later on, but already the contrast in 2:1–2, 8–20 is striking: the Savior–Messiah-Lord enters the world of Augustus, but this "good news" is not for his ears, but for the shepherds. The coming of this baby is good news for peasants, not rulers (cf. 1:52–53).

Luke spends more time presenting status-markers for Zechariah (1:5–7, 9), Elizabeth (1:5–7, 25, 41, 58), and Joseph (1:27; 2:22–24). Simeon and Anna are similarly introduced (2:25, 36–37) and, in the context of turn-of-the-era temple piety, they are well presented. Elsewhere, banquet guests are concerned with who gets invited and what position at the meal one occupies – both markers of status in Greco-Roman Palestine (14:7–14); and the teachers of the law are said to manifest their concern with status by their clothing, seats in the synagogue, and the like (20:46–47). As we will see, especially consequen-

---

[19] See M.I. Finley, *The Ancient Economy*, SCL 43 (Berkeley: University of California Press, 1973) 50–51; Joel B. Green, "Good News to Whom? Jesus and the 'Poor' in the Gospel of Luke," in *Jesus of Nazareth: Lord and Christ. Essays on the Historical Jesus and New Testament Christology*, ed. Joel B. Green and Max Turner (Grand Rapids, Michigan: Wm. B. Eerdmans, 1994) 59–74.

tial in Luke is *status reversal*, together with Luke's concern to redefine the basis by which status is determined.

Fourth, the Gospel of Luke opens and closes with an acknowledgment of *the centrality of the Jerusalem temple* to the social world of Jesus. This and other material emphasizes for us the importance of *the piety of Israel* in Luke's account. As the character references given for Zechariah and Elizabeth (1:5–7) and especially the presentation of Jesus in the temple (2:22–39; especially v. 39) stress, Luke is concerned to show the importance of faithful obedience. This obedience is directed to the law, the validity of which is thus assumed in the birth narrative, even if this perspective will receive further development later in the Gospel. Obedience is also extended to the words of the angel, who speaks on God's behalf (cf. 1:13 → 1:59–63; 1:31 → 2:21), and the requirements of the Abrahamic covenant (1:59; 2:21). Moreover, portraits of Jewish piety appear in references to prayer, worship, fasting, and expectant waiting (e.g., 1:10, 13, 25, 46–55, 69–79; 2:13, 14, 20, 25, 37, 38) – and, indeed, to the representation of life oriented around the Jerusalem temple (e.g., 1:8–10, 21–23; 2:22–51). In this world, we are breathing the air of first-century Palestinian Jewish piety.[20]

In the light of the importance of the temple in the Third Gospel, the balance between the temple and the house in Luke 1–2 is noteworthy. There, *both* function as space for divine revelation and the praise of God (1:26–56). As the narrative develops, a similar pairing of synagogue and house will occur. In the end, temple and synagogue will present themselves as antagonist to Jesus and his message, and the house will more and more become the center of Jesus' movement.

Finally, in this attempt to draw attention to key aspects of Jesus' world in the Gospel of Luke, we may note the emphasis Luke places on *rural and urban life*. Galilee is the locus of Jesus' ministry until he begins the long, wandering journey to Jerusalem in 9:51. Even in these opening chapters of Jesus' public

---

[20] Cf. Joseph B. Tyson, *Images of Judaism in Luke–Acts* (Columbia: University of South Carolina Press, 1992) 42–55; E. P. Sanders, *Judaism: Practice and Belief, 63 BCE–66CE* (London: SCM; Philadelphia: Trinity, 1992) 53.

ministry, however, the reach of Jesus' reputation and mission extends beyond the borders of Galilee (cf. 5:16; 6:17).

"Galilee" is more than a geographical location, and it is important to ask how this spatial marker locates the story on the cultural map. Galilee (together with Jericho) was the heart of agricultural production in Palestine. Its fertile soil contributed to the growth of such crops as grapes (for wine), figs, olives, and wheat, as well as to pasturage, while the Sea of Galilee served as the hub of an important fishing industry.[21] This was an agrarian society marked by many features of peasant culture. One encounters, for example, agriculture-related settings for Jesus' ministry (5:1–11; 6:1; 8:32) and parabolic teaching (8:5–8); indeed, peasant life provides a metaphorical arsenal for his instruction – see, for example, 5:37–38; 6:38, 41–44, 48–49; 7:32; 8:5–8, 18.

Socio-economic realities among Galilean peasantry, in part grounded in and fueled by disaffection toward Roman occupation, contributed to social unrest in the region. Although Hellenization was influential throughout the land of the Jews by the first century CE, this was apparently less so in the sparsely populated area of upper Galilee. In some ways, then, this area was "beyond the easy reach" of a more pervasive Hellenism and, for practical purposes, was outside the firm grip of Roman overlordship. Historically, the story here was one of stubborn resistance to alien cultural influence and foreign domination.

Peasant societies typically evidence a general (though not absolute) polarity between the city (locus of power, wealth, and privilege) and the village/countryside (rural populace of peasants). Within Luke's Galilee, however, such a distinction has no place. In fact, a survey of Luke's language of the city, village, and country reveals that Luke is relatively indiscriminate in his use of such categories. Galilean cities are not characterized as the habitats of the power elite who trouble

---

[21] See Josephus, *J.W.* 3.3.1–2 §§35–43; 3.10.8 §§516–21. See Rainer Riesner, "Galilee," in *DJG*, 252–53; Douglas E. Oakman, "The Countryside in Luke–Acts," in Neyrey, ed., *Social World*; Sean Freyne, *Galilee, Jesus and the Gospels: Literary Approaches and Historical Investigations* (Philadelphia: Fortress, 1988) 90–115.

Jesus. Resistance can arise in the city (4:29, 31), but so can the city serve as a place of retreat (9:10). The presence of the power elite in the Galilean ministry of Jesus is mostly indirect – as in the mention of a toll office (5:27), and the allusion to Tiberius, Herod's home, in 7:18 (cf. 3:19–20); 9:7–9.

When Jesus first encounters hostility from the power-brokers of his people, it is significant that they have been joined by their colleagues from outside Galilee – that is, from Judea and, especially, from the city of Jerusalem (5:17; cf. Acts 14:19). That Jerusalem is singled out in 5:17 is not only evidence of its geo-political and socio-religious importance in ancient Palestine, but also serves proleptically to identify the Jewish leaders from Jerusalem as the primary group hostile to Jesus.

In other ways Luke's narrative reflects more straight-forwardly what would be expected in an agrarian culture, especially as this relates to economics. First, peasant existence generally is characterized by the ever-present demands of one's family, the needs of one's ongoing agricultural operation, and the requirements of the state, in this case, Rome. Peasant life, then, rests uneasily on a narrow margin between subsistence and abject poverty, and it is against such a background that gleaning rights (6:1) and a feeding miracle (9:12–17) might gain special significance. Moreover, this underlines the unwelcome presence of toll-collectors like Levi and his friends (5:27, 29) and indicates how far Jesus will go to exemplify his message of good news to the socially despised.

Second, we may refer to systems of economic exchange within the peasant village, of which two sorts were operative. The first is generalized reciprocity – that is, a transaction characteristic of those who share close kinship ties, whereby the exchange is essentially one-sided, altruistic, the giving of a gift without explicit stipulations for any reciprocation in kind. The second is balanced reciprocity – the direct exchange of goods of approximately equal value within a relatively narrow period of time.[22] Concerns with reciprocity are present in Luke's

---

[22] For these concepts and especially the relation of kinship distance to reciprocity variation, see Marshall Sahlins, *Stone Age Economics* (London/New York: Routledge, 1972) 185–230.

account – e.g., "the measure you give will be the measure you get back" (6:38c) – and can be brought to the forefront in order to be dismissed or parodied. Here, it is important to observe the central role allotted to kinship relations, evaluations of social distance and nearness, in peasant life. Characters in Luke's account show a marked concern for determining the boundaries of "our group" and stipulating the nature of appropriate interaction with those outside the group (e.g., 4:23–29; 9:49–50). Numerous factors can contribute to the definitions of acceptable limits in kinship-based cultures, including physical maladies which are marks of uncleanness (e.g., 14:21) or keep one from making the expected contribution to village subsistence. Jesus not only condemns the way this concern with boundaries is manifested, but himself engages in practices such as extending forgiveness and healing that restore community status (e.g., 4:18–19, 39; 5:14; 7:15, 34, 36–50; 9:12–17; 13:10–17).

Third, and closely related, Luke's narrative reflects the patronage system characteristic of the Mediterranean world – a system of relationships grounded in inequality between the two principals:

A patron has social, economic, and political resources that are needed by a client. In return, a client can give expressions of loyalty and honor that are useful for the patron.[23]

A textbook case example of patronage appears in 7:1–10 where Jesus is approached by some Jewish elders sent by a centurion who needs Jesus' help. According to the elders (i.e., the clients), the centurion (i.e., the patron) deserves Jesus' help since he built the synagogue in Capernaum. Overall, however, Luke's accounts are less focused on individual patron–client relations and less friendly toward the institution of patronage. In fact, Luke's material is more concerned with the patronal system as such, a system by means of which those in need

---

[23] Halvor Moxnes, "Patron–Client Relations and the New Community in Luke–Acts," in Neyrey, ed., *Social World*, 241–68 (242). See also *Patrons and Clients in Mediterranean Societies*, ed. Ernest Gellner and John Waterbury (London: Duckworth, 1977).

(clients) are controlled by those (patrons) to whom they are indebted. Of special interest, then, is Jesus' instruction to give without expectation of return – a message applicable to patronal relations and to systems of balanced reciprocity – in 6:34–35, together with his portrayal of God as the Supreme Benefactor who gives freely (6:35b-36). In these contexts it is imperative to remember that Jesus thus makes an economic statement grounded ultimately in his vision of a transformed system of social relations. People who follow Jesus are to give to each other as they would to those of their immediate kinship group. Distinctions based on social status as defined in the larger world are thus overturned as Jesus challenges people to accept the previously unacceptable as though they were family.

By now, the degree to which cultural realities and theological and ethical outlooks are interrelated in Luke's world is clear. Also evident is the degree to which cultural realities, such as Jewish piety and Roman occupation, are themselves tightly interwoven in the world of Jesus according to Luke. Religion, economics, politics, group identity – these and other such social ingredients are closely interwoven, not presumed to be separate as they often are at present. We must keep this ever before us as we explore further the narrative theology of the Third Evangelist.

THEOPHILUS AND LUKE'S "NARRATIVE"

(1) Since many have undertaken to set down an orderly account of the events that have been fulfilled among us, (2) just as they were handed down to us by those who from the beginning were eye-witnesses and servants of the word, (3) I too decided, after investigating everything carefully from the very first, to write an orderly account for you, most excellent Theophilus, (4) so that you may know the truth concerning the things about which you have been informed. (Luke 1:1–4)

What sort of knowledge might Luke have presumed on the part of his audience? This is a question, first, about the sort of general background Luke will have shared with his audience. He assumes, for example, a Greek-speaking audience, inclusive of persons capable of reading the language sometimes in Classical, sometimes in Septuagintal style. And he assumes and builds on such "inside" cultural awareness as we have been outlining. Second, it is a question more specifically about the knowledge shared in Luke's more particular discourse situation. He is not writing to the Greco-Roman population in general; rather, his Gospel grows out of and speaks to more focused Christian concerns. Our knowledge of those concerns can be derived only in conversation with Luke's writing itself.

One important way of framing the question would be to explore what sort of writing "The Gospel of Luke" is. Although, following Christian tradition since the early second century, we have learned to call the first four books in our New Testament "Gospels," it is worth remembering that no such genre or form of writing existed in Luke's day. The question of the genre of Luke is important, for prior decisions about the sort of literature one is reading predetermine to some degree the lens through which one comes to understand that literature. And for decisions about the genre of Luke, the opening four verses, 1:1–4, are instrumental. For writers in antiquity, where the first column of writing, even the first sentence, performed much of the purpose of the modern book-jacket blurb, table of contents, and title page, a literary work's opening sentence was crucial for alerting those who either read it or heard it read to what could be expected in the work as a whole.[24]

If Luke's audience would not immediately have recognized his work as a "Gospel," how might it have been taken? A broad consensus has emerged in this century that Luke 1:1–4, and with it the whole Lukan project, belongs within the literary tradition of ancient historiography. Against this identification the primary dissenting voice has been raised by those who find the closest generic parallels for Luke in Greco-Roman biography.[25] It has also been argued that the closest stylistic ana-

---

[24] Cf. Donald Earl, "Prologue-form in Ancient Historiography," *ANRW* 1.2:842–56.
[25] Most recently, Richard A. Burridge, *What Are the Gospels? A Comparison with Graeco-Roman Biography*, SNTSMS 70 (Cambridge University Press, 1992).

logues to Luke 1:1–4 are in the "scientific tradition" of technical writing on mathematics, engineering, and the like.[26] These alternatives exploit the formal differences between Luke's preface and those of the Greek historiographers. On the other hand, Luke 1:1–4 and Acts 1:1 share many common features with the prefaces to the first-century CE work of the Jewish historian Josephus, *Against Apion*, also in two volumes (see 1.1 §§1–5; 2.1 §§1–2), as well as many other features of Greco-Roman historiography – e.g., a genealogical record (Luke 3:23–28); the use of meal scenes as occasions for instruction (as in Greco-Roman symposia); travel narratives; speeches; letters; and dramatic episodes, such as Jesus' rejection at Nazareth (4:16–30), and Paul's stormy voyage and shipwreck (Acts 27:1–28:14).[27]

Moreover, in describing his work as a narrative (διήγησις), Luke identifies his project as an account of many events, for which the chief prototypes were the early Greek histories of Herodotus and Thucydides.[28] Further, that Luke–Acts does not match in every instance the formal features of Greco-Roman historiography presents no immediate problem, for Luke has been influenced as well by Old Testament and Jewish historiography, especially with respect to the use of historical sequences to shape a narrative theology. What is clear is that Luke, perhaps more than the other Evangelists, has been influenced by Greco-Roman literary forms – especially those related to the biographical genre, even if other formal features and above all the theocentric focus of his narrative preclude identification of Luke–Acts as "biography."[29]

[26] Alexander, *Preface*; Alexander, "Luke's Preface."

[27] David E. Aune, *The New Testament in Its Literary Environment*, LEC (Philadelphia: Westminster, 1987) 120–31.

[28] Cf. Hermogenes *Progymnasmata* 2; Lucian *How to Write History* §55: "For all the body of the history is simply a long narrative" (διήγησις μακρά).

[29] For critiques of the biographical identification of the Gospels, see Robert Guelich, "The Gospel Genre," in *Das Evangelium und die Evangelien: Vorträge vom Tübinger Symposium 1982*, ed. Peter Stuhlmacher, WUNT 28 (Tübingen: J. C. B. Mohr [Paul Siebeck], 1983) 183–219; Albrecht Dihle, "Die Evangelien und die griechische Biographie," in *Das Evangelium und die Evangelien*, ed. Stuhlmacher, 383–411; Larry W. Hurtado, "Gospel (Genre)," in *DJG*, 276–82. See also Joel B. Green, *The Gospel of Luke*, NICNT (Grand Rapids, Michigan: Wm. B. Eerdmans, forthcoming).

What does it mean to refer to Luke's writing as "historiography"? This question has been problematized by attempts to read back into antiquity modern notions of historical veracity. Luke himself addresses this issue in two ways in his preface. First, Luke presents his work as "an orderly account" (διήγη-σις). It has been suggested that Luke is drawing on the rhetorical tradition for this usage, and is thus interested in a "longer narrative composed of a number of events," arranged "by the display of major developments and patterns."[30] We should go on to notice Luke's use of the cognate verb, "to narrate, to give an account" (διηγέομαι), which he characteristically employs for the act of describing God's mighty deeds (Luke 8:39; 9:10; Acts 9:27; 12:17). For Luke, "narrative" is proclamation. Luke has in mind the use of history to preach, to set forth a persuasive, narrative interpretation of God's work in Jesus.

Second, Luke appears in his preface to make a strong claim about the "certainty" of the account to follow, but this must not be read as an attempt to drive a wedge between "history" and "interpretation." For Luke, the narrative is not an historical or other basis for proclamation; rather, narration is proclamation. Luke's terminology suggests "the convincing nature of his presentation"[31] or "the certainty of these things" (cf. Acts 2:36; 25:26). So, while the Christian message is inseparably tied to the historical events related to its origins and progression, and Luke must therefore necessarily be concerned with "what happened,"[32] the question of interpretation is vital for him. Increasingly we have learned not to pose the historian's task with questions such as, how can the past be objectively captured? or what methods will allow the recovery of "what actually happened"? Historiography imposes significance on the past already by its choice of events to record

---

[30] Robert C. Tannehill, *The Narrative Unity of Luke–Acts: A Literary Interpretation*, vol. 1: *The Gospel According to Luke*, FF (Philadelphia: Fortress, 1986) 10.

[31] Cf. Xenophon *Memorabilia* 4.6 §15; Colin Brown, "ἀσφάλεια," *NIDNTT* 1:663.

[32] See the use of ἀσφαλής in Acts 21:34; 22:30 to signify "the facts" in a case. Cf. Roger Trigg, "'Tales Artfully Spun'," in *The Bible as Rhetoric: Studies in Biblical Persuasion and Credibility*, ed. Martin Warner, WSPL (London: Routledge, 1990) 117–32.

and to order as well as by its inherent efforts to postulate for those events an end and/or origin. The emphasis thus shifts from validation to signification.[33] The issue is, how is the past being represented? Luke's concern with truth, then, resides above all in his interpretation of the past.

A further issue of presupposition is raised by Luke's preface, for it refers to the existence of literary predecessors as if these were well known to his audience. Unfortunately, their shared knowledge is not ours, with the result that, on the basis of evidence internal to the Third Gospel, we can only speculate as to their nature and, especially, as to whether Luke's predecessors included in their number one or more of our New Testament Gospels. Greater certainty on this issue might better satisfy our curiosity concerning the development of Christian writing in earliest times, but Luke's reference to his predecessors probably has a separate purpose – namely, to vouch for the value of his "undertaking" through appeal to his association with the tradition.

Although most Gospels scholars continue to believe Luke knew and used Mark's Gospel as a source,[34] a vocal minority assert Luke's primary use of Matthew's Gospel.[35] Assuming Luke's audience, unlike modern redaction critics, possessed neither the materials nor curiosity to investigate Luke's use of his source(s) word by word or line by line, for a theological appreciation of Luke's work the assertion of this relationship·to his predecessors is nevertheless of importance. First, this is one of the primary means by which he advances his authority and elicits a positive hearing. Luke's narrative is thus itself inscribed into the chain of tradition represented "by those who from the beginning were eyewitnesses and servants of the

---

[33] See Hayden White, *The Content and the Form: Narrative Discourse and Historical Representation* (Baltimore: Johns Hopkins University Press, 1987); Linda Hutcheon, *A Poetics of Postmodernism: History, Theory, Fiction* (New York: Routledge, 1988) esp. 20, 88–101, 124–5, 128; Brian Stock, *Listening for the Text: On the Uses of the Past*, PRCS (Baltimore: Johns Hopkins University Press, 1990).

[34] For a summary of this position and bibliography, see Robert H. Stein, "Synoptic Problem," in *DJG*, 784–92.

[35] Impetus for this alternative has been provided in modern times by William R. Farmer, *The Synoptic Problem: A Critical Analysis* (Macon, Georgia: Mercer University Press, 1976).

word." Second, we must assume that he expected his readers and auditors to recognize some or all of the episodes of his Gospel; hence, his chief contribution as a narrative theologian would be recognized not only in whatever fresh material he was able to include, but also and especially in his ordering and staging of the account.[36]

We have suggested, then, that an appreciation of the theology of the Gospel of Luke is predicated especially on (1) grappling with the ways Luke has interacted with the world of Greco-Roman Palestine, and (2) exploring the particular shaping he has given his narrative. We will see the major role given to the Scriptures of Israel in this narrative theology. We will also lay bare how traditional scenes with Jesus as their central character have been shaped internally and staged in relation to others so as to communicate *both* in the sense of passing on information *and* in the sense of calling forth a response on the part of Luke's audience. Luke, we will see, is concerned fundamentally that people align themselves with the redemptive aim of God and serve this aim, just as Jesus has done. Indeed, Jesus' life, death, resurrection, and anticipated parousia combine to reveal – i.e., to show and to make present, and thus to make possible – God's overarching salvific purpose and the way of humans to share in that purpose as recipients and as agents of divine deliverance.

---

[36] Clues to these theological interests may be uncovered by means of redaction criticism, the exploration of the Evangelist's amendments to the tradition(s) he has received, but these clues must be tested against the emphases of the narrative as a whole.

CHAPTER 2

"God my Savior":
the purpose of God in Luke's Gospel

The Gospel of Luke narrates the long-awaited intervention and determined activity of God to accomplish his historic purpose. In Luke's rendering of this redemptive project, God is joined by others – both human and spiritual – working either to embrace and serve or to reject and oppose his aim.

This is good story-telling: the highlighting of a problem requiring a solution, the resulting motif of conflict raising readers' interest, building tension, and pushing the story along toward its climax.[1] For Luke, though, this is much more than a good story. For him, this is the way things "were" and "are," for the divine purpose and the conflict to which Luke's account bears witness was at the time of his writing still ongoing. Situated in the latter third of the first century CE, he relates the story of Jesus for more than entertainment, just as he does so for more than antiquarian interest or fidelity. His is an engaged and engaging accounting of the ministry of Jesus and Christian beginnings.

The struggle to achieve the divine aim Luke recounts did not reach its resolution in the Third Gospel, but spilled over into the activity of the Jesus-movement in Acts. In an important sense, then, Acts is grounded in the Gospel of Luke, just as the Gospel is grounded in God's purpose as related in Israel's Scriptures. What is more, the aim of God, by the end of Acts, had still not reached its consummation; nor had it done so by the time of Luke's own writing. Nor has it yet. As one who

---

[1] Cf., e.g., Mieke Bal, *Narratology: Introduction to the Theory of Narrative* (University of Toronto Press, 1985) 30–31.

preaches with history, then, the Third Evangelist presents the story of the Messiah's coming into the world and the conflict engendered by this divine visitation so as to invite response from his audience. With whom will his readers and auditors side? Will they reject God's purpose, like those Pharisees and teachers of the law Luke describes in 7:30? Or will they follow the toll-collectors of 7:29, acknowledging God's justice, orienting their lives around his project in the world (cf. 3:12–13)?

In fact, periodically Luke slows the pace of his narrative, sometimes even brings it to a halt, in order to invite his audience to reflect on its development. On the one hand, Luke invites contemplation on *the significance* of "these events." "Are you the one who is to come?" John's disciples ask (7:19), interjecting into the drama a review of Jesus' divine commission in terms borrowed from his inaugural address (7:18–22; cf. 4:18–19). Yes, he is the one, and the divine mission he serves and embodies is oriented to those in great need. "John I beheaded, so who is this about whom I am hearing such things?" Herod asks (9:9), again inviting reflection on the nature of Jesus' mission. He is the one who has compassion on the hungry thousands *and* who has power from God to provide food for them, and this prepares for Peter's declaration, "[You are] the Messiah of God" (9:20). Luke invites his readers and auditors into what we might call hermeneutical asides (e.g., the Song of Mary [1:46–55]) in order to encourage growth in understanding, then, but also to provide opportunity for their own responses to this divine invitation. Will their responses follow that of Zechariah – hesitant, questioning (1:18) – or Mary – willing, submissive, pondering (1:29, 38)? Subsequent readers, too, are invited to embrace a perspective internal to the narrative, and thus to explore for themselves how they might be aligning themselves *vis-à-vis* God's purpose.

In other words, the Third Gospel must be understood as serving more than a *representational* function. It does perform in this way – that is, to pass on information about the birth, ministry, death, and resurrection of Jesus. But it is also and more significantly an instrument of *communication* – that is, it seeks to involve its readers and auditors in an interactive discourse with the intention of realizing particular aims.[2] Specifically, the Third Gospel encourages its audience to recognize, and having recognized, to embrace and to serve the salvific aim of God. According to Luke's Gospel, God purposes to bring salvation in all of its fullness to all persons. But, as becomes immediately clear already in the birth narrative of Luke 1–2, this is not an aim that will be reached easily or without resistance. It requires the affirmative and committed responses of people like Elizabeth, Mary, Simeon, Anna, and others (both in the narrative and outside of it), for God's aim necessarily involves the collusion of human actors.

The agenda we have set for ourselves in this chapter is to explore more fully this divine project – both its content and the means by which it is communicated and furthered in the Third Gospel. As we do, we must take account of the reality that not all respond favorably to God's aim – nor, more specifically, to God's agent of salvation, Jesus. This gives rise to antagonism, division, and conflict.

LUKE AND THE SCRIPTURES

One of the primary, but by no means the only, means by which Luke evidences his interest in the divine plan is his deployment of the Scriptures of Israel. This may seem surprising to some readers of the Third Gospel, since direct citations are not plentiful and special attention is not often drawn to the specific fulfillment of scriptural texts as in, say, Matthew's Gospel. Important citations do appear in Luke, though, and at highly significant locations. Of even greater significance than the explicit use of the Scriptures is their appearance implicitly, in the form of summary references to "the law and the prophets" or, more pervasively, woven into the warp and woof of the narrative presentation of Jesus' ministry.

We can easily demonstrate the strategic placement of scriptural quotations in the Lukan narrative. For example, in 3:4–6

---

[2] Cf. Jean Caron, *An Introduction to Psycholinguistics* (University of Toronto Press, 1992) 125–69 (149).

and 4:18–19 citations from Isaiah are employed at the outset of
the public ministries of John and Jesus by way of defining the
shape and purpose of their ministries. The Scriptures supply
the salvation-historical framework for understanding their
respective missions and so root their activity in the ongoing
story of God's redemptive work. The enigma of the suffering of
Jesus, Son of God, Messiah, and the coming resistance to be
faced by Jesus' disciples are addressed straightforwardly in two
citations in the Lukan passion narrative. Referring to Isa.
53:12, Jesus, in Luke 22:37, grounds not only his own fate but
also that of his followers in Isaianic prophecy. And in 23:46,
Jesus identifies in his death with the Righteous Sufferer of Ps.
31:5.

Of perhaps greater consequence for our appreciation of
Luke's use of the Scriptures of Israel are the less obvious but
nonetheless extensive use of scriptural echoes. Interpreters of
Luke's Gospel have long noted the septuagintal "feel" of the
infancy narratives of Luke 1:5–2:52; more recently, attention
has been drawn to the multiplicity of ways Luke "inscribes"
the story of Jesus into the ongoing story of God's purpose in the
Scriptures. If "context" refers to the socio-historical realities in
which the Lukan text is set, and if "co-text" refers to the
relationship of a Lukan text to the larger Lukan narrative, then
"intertext" refers to yet another interpretive horizon by which
we interpret Luke's writing.[3] Like all literature, Luke's Gospel
draws on other texts, for Luke especially those of the Greek
version of what we have come to call the Old Testament. By
this form of intertextuality, he locates his narrative in those
texts so as to allow the significance of the "old story" to shed
light on the present one, just as the story of Jesus, then, is
allowed to interpret the story of Israel.

---

[3] On intertextuality, see Jonathan Culler, *The Pursuit of Signs: Semiotics, Literature,
Deconstruction* (London: Routledge and Kegan Paul, 1991) esp. ch. 5; Michael
Worton and Judith Sill, eds., *Intertextuality: Theories and Practices* (Manchester University
Press, 1990); esp. "Introduction" (1–44). On intertextuality and biblical
studies, see Daniel Boyarin, *Intertextuality and the Reading of Midrash*, ISBL (Bloomington/Indianapolis:
Indiana University Press, 1990); Richard B. Hays, *Echoes of
Scripture in the Letters of Paul* (New Haven/London: Yale University Press, 1989);
William Vorster, "Intertextuality and Redaktionsgeschichte," in *Intertextuality in*

What theological agenda might be served by the use of the Scriptures in this way? First, it is transparent that the rich interplay of scriptural texts within the story of Jesus roots that story in the authoritative story of Israel. As Acts 13:17–23 indicates, the coming of Jesus was nothing less than the next step in the God–Israel relationship by which God would redeem his people. Second, this intertextuality reveals the oneness of God's aim; the same purpose is being served, the one story is ongoing – now in the ministry of Jesus and those who follow Jesus. Third, the possibility of parody is thus introduced, so that Luke can draw attention to similarities between the present and past, while at the same time underscoring dissimilarities. This is of major importance for Luke because of his belief that what is happening in and through Jesus is not only the unfolding but indeed the fulfillment of God's design, witnessed in the Scriptures. We may illustrate this way of hearing the Scriptures in Luke's narrative with reference to the story of the testing of Jesus.

Questions of *identity* – specifically the nature of Jesus' identity as *Son of God* – are at the fore in Luke 4:1–13, where the Scriptures are also cited. In this case, though, it is interesting that both Jesus and the devil cite the Scriptures, and to different ends. This example has special importance because it shows (1) Luke's fondness for the use of *echoes* of Scripture in addition to his interest in actually citing biblical texts, and (2) the degree to which *Scripture alone* cannot serve for Luke as testimony to God's purpose. The narrator sets Jesus' encounter with the devil in a formidable interpretive context – namely, the testing of Israel in the wilderness. One might notice such evidences of intertextuality as the following:

divine leading in the wilderness (Deut. 8:2; cf. Luke 4:1);
"forty" (Exod. 16:35; Num. 14:34; Deut. 8:2, 4; cf. Luke 4:2);
Israel as God's son (e.g., Exod. 4:22–23; cf. Luke 4:3, 9);
parallel testing, with the scriptural texts Jesus cites deriving

Biblical Writings: Essays in Honour of Bas van Iersel, ed. Sipke Draisma (Kampen: Uitgeversmaatschappij J. K. Kok, 1989) 15–26.

from those events in which Israel was tested by God (Deut. 6–8); and

whereas Jesus was full of the Spirit and followed the Spirit's guidance, Israel "rebelled and grieved his holy spirit" (Isa. 63:10).

And still other echoes might be heard. According to Deuteronomy, (1) Israel was allowed to hunger in order to learn that one does not live by bread alone (8:3); (2) Israel was instructed to worship the one and only God, and not to follow after any other god (6:4–15); and (3) Israel was commanded not to put the Lord God to the test (6:16). In each case, however, Israel failed in its obedience to God (e.g., Exod. 17:1–7; Deut. 9:6–29; cf. Acts 7:35, 39–43). Luke thus draws together a virtual choir of voices to tell this story and to give it significance. Jesus is presented in his representative role as Israel, God's son. No sooner are these resemblances sensed than the remarkable discontinuities assert themselves, however, for unlike Israel, Jesus proved his fidelity in the wilderness. He is the faithful Son of God.

Moving from the first and second temptations to the third, we are now aware that Jesus' ears are attuned to the voice of God. The devil shares in this recognition, and so adopts a different strategy. He attempts now to speak with God's own voice (4:9–10; cf. Ps. 91:11–12). Because the devil is not a reliable character in the Gospel of Luke, we might be tempted simply to dismiss his use of the Scriptures as duplicitous. But this does not address the hermeneutical quandary here. Both Jesus and the devil quote Scripture; why prefer one reading over the other?

Fundamentally, the issue here is related to Jesus' radical commitment to the one aim of God, God's eschatological agenda. The devil introduces an alternative aim, a competing agenda. He wants to recruit Jesus to participate in a test of the divine promises of Psalm 91. In doing so, the devil overlooks the crucial factor that the psalm is addressed to those who are known for their fidelity to God; that is, even in the psalm faithful obedience to God is the controlling need. Jesus, then, does not deny the validity of God's promises as quoted by the devil, but rejects the suitability of their appropriation in this context. He recognizes the devil's strategy as an attempt to deflect him from his single-minded commitment to loyalty and obedience in God's service, and interprets the devil's invitation as an encouragement to question God's faithfulness. Israel had manifested its doubts by testing God, but Jesus refuses to do so (cf. Deut. 6:16).

This encounter points to a larger reality in the Gospel of Luke – namely, that the aim of God is even more key to Luke than are the Scriptures of Israel. To put it another way, the Scriptures are of importance for Luke particularly because they witness to God's purpose, and they are interpreted correctly *by* those who are unswervingly committed to God's purpose and in line with the purpose of God. For Luke, the Scriptures provide the storyline for the working out of the divine purpose of God, which has yet to be fulfilled. The story of the realization of God's aim is still being written. The myriads of scriptural echoes we may hear in the background of Luke's narrative of Jesus' ministry encourage the reader to adopt Luke's perspective: The story of God's purpose has not drawn to a close but, quite the contrary, is manifestly still being written in the life of Jesus – then, in Acts, in the life of the early Christian communities, and is now ongoing. Luke thus invites his readers to join him in reading the Scriptures and their ongoing story in the life of Jesus and the early church so as to identify the redemptive aim of God and, then, to embrace and serve it.

GOD'S DESIGN

The Third Evangelist draws on a metaphorical arsenal in his attempt to communicate the arrival and ministry of Jesus as the actualization of God's redemptive plan in history. Inasmuch as John serves very much as the forerunner of Jesus in the early chapters of Luke's Gospel, we must recognize that his arrival and ministry, too, manifest the divine intention. This is clear in three ways. First, for Luke, *that* John and Jesus arrive on the scene *at all* is itself a revelation of God's gracious design.

Their coming into the world is the consequence of divine intervention. The births of these two sons are grounded in and already bring to fruition the ancient promises of God. Second, it is especially true of Jesus that we see him deliberately embracing the divine project – exercising his own volition and acting in ways that advance God's aim. Luke portrays Jesus as one actively engaged in discerning the will of God so as to take steps toward its consummation. Third, as a consequence of the ministry first of John, then of Jesus, others are summoned to orient themselves around God's purpose. Thus they are urged to participate in God's project both as recipients and as agents of his graciousness. Within Luke's Gospel, John and Jesus are not following their own agenda; behind their missions and message stands the one purpose of God – sometimes lurking just beneath the surface of the narrative, but brought repeatedly into the limelight.

We may discern Luke's interest in the design of God by attending to a series of expressive terms – especially βουλή ("purpose"), βούλομαι ("to want"), δεῖ ("it is necessary"), θέλημα ("will"), θέλω ("to will"), ὁρίζω ("to determine"), πληρόω ("to fulfill"), and προφήτης ("prophet"). These are not technical terms for Luke, nor is each developed in a discrete way by the Evangelist.[4] Rather, employed in a variety of co-texts, they help shape an understanding of God and God's purpose that occupies a central place in the theology of the Gospel of Luke.

The ancient plan

Luke roots the story of Jesus in the ancient plan. This important Lukan motif is present already in the Gospel's opening verse, in the phrase: "an orderly account of the events that have been fulfilled[5] among us" (1:1). The phrase with which

---

[4] Cf. Charles H. Cosgrove, "The Divine ΔΕΙ in Luke–Acts: Investigations into the Lukan Understanding of God's Providence," *NovT* 26 (1984) 168–90; Gerhardus Petrus Viljoen du Plooy, "The Narrative Act in Luke–Acts from the Perspective of God's Design" (Th.D. diss., University of Stellenbosch, 1986); John T. Squires, *The Plan of God in Luke–Acts*, SNTSMS 76 (Cambridge University Press, 1993).

[5] Πληροφορέω appears only here in Luke and is a synonym for πληρόω.

Luke modifies "events" – "that have been fulfilled among us"
– indicates that these events are incomplete in themselves but
must be understood within some antecedent web of activity.
Indeed, writers of narrative inevitably struggle with locating a
beginning point sufficient to show how what follows grows out
of narrated exigencies. Luke's struggle, it would appear, led
him to a double solution. On the one hand, the "beginning" of
his narrative is located in the births of John and Jesus
(1:5–2:52). On the other, even these events are grounded in
something prior – namely, God's purpose, evident in Israel's
Scriptures and the history of God's people, as its culmination.
As Mary proclaims, with the promise of the birth of the Son of
God, "[God] has helped his servant Israel, in remembrance of
his mercy, just as he announced to our ancestors . . . ."
(1:54–55). This is not to say that the Lukan prologue is concerned with a narrow understanding of "prophetic fulfillment." Rather, the Evangelist is concerned to show that this
"new" story, the story of Jesus, joins the "old," scriptural story
as its ongoing manifestation and, indeed, as the realization of
God's ancient plan.[6]

This motif is furthered by Luke's numerous references to
"the Scriptures" (see above) and, more specifically, to "the
prophets." In the miraculous events of the birth stories, Zechariah recognizes God's acting in a way consistent with his
promises through the ancient prophets (1:70), just as Luke
himself situates the ministry of John in the prophetic words of
Isaiah (3:3–6). In 4:21, Jesus announces that the inception of
his own public ministry is the fulfillment (πληρόω) of scripture;
similarly, following his resurrection, he remarks to his disciples
that the law of Moses, the prophets, and the psalms spoke of
him, and that what they said concerning him "must be fulfilled" (δεῖ + πληρόω; cf. 22:37; 24:25–26). Indeed, for Luke
the ministry of Jesus is incomprehensible apart from its

---

[6] On Luke 1:1, cf. François Bovon, *Das Evangelium nach Lukas*, vol. 1, EKKNT 3.1
   (Zurich: Benziger; Neukirchen-Vluyn: Neukirchener, 1989) 35. More generally, cf.
   Joel B. Green, "The Problem of a Beginning: Israel's Scriptures in Luke 1–2," *BBR* 4
   (1994) 1–25. Thus, the modifier, "have been fulfilled," should be read as a divine
   passive, with God as its unspoken subject.

interpretive relation to "the scriptures" (cf., e.g., 24:44–49; 16:29–31).[7]

Luke's interest in the ancient plan serves two noticeable roles. First, by means of this motif Luke ties the story of Jesus into the story of Israel; they are bound together in hermeneutical association so that Luke's audience is advised to return again and again to the Scriptures of Israel in order to appreciate more fully the significance of the story of Jesus. Second, grounding the story of Jesus in the story of God's purpose serves a legitimating function. The rejection of Jesus already in Nazareth (after Jesus' declaration of the fulfillment of scripture "today," "in your hearing" [4:21]) is only one of many clues that the mission of Jesus presents obstacles to its potential recipients. Had not Simeon already warned that Jesus was destined for the falling and rising of many in Israel (2:34)? In fact, the degree to which Luke repeatedly emphasizes that the Messiah's death is nothing other than what was anticipated by the ancient plan of God only evidences how hard it would have been to understand God's purpose having come to expression in this way. Luke's theology of the cross thus constitutes an oxymoron. Some characters within the narrative refuse to believe that in Jesus God has graciously visited his people. In the ongoing story of the Jesus movement, in Acts and subsequently, the response to the "good news" was not (and has not been) uniformly positive. How could this be God's will? Could one who serves God's aim encounter such opposition? Repeated reminders of the continued outworking of the overarching aim of God provide a divine sanction for the story as Luke tells it. Strange as it may appear at times, this is, after all, *God's story.*

Opposition to God's purpose

According to Luke's presentation, the reason God's purpose is not embraced universally is that other purposes are also at work. A second motif to which the terminological evidence of

---

[7] See Richard J. Dillon, *From Eye-Witnesses to Ministers of the Word: Tradition and Composition in Luke 24*, AnBib 82 (Rome: Biblical Institute, 1978).

God's design in the Third Gospel points, then, is *the presence of contrasting aims*. Some earlier study of divine providence concerned itself with an alleged Lukan concern with divine determinism, as though God's purpose were a *fait accompli*.[8] On the macro-level, it is certainly true for Luke that the will of God will be done. Beyond this general, albeit important affirmation, however, a theology of divine determinism makes little sense of the Lukan narrative. *What* God purposes may be known. *That* what God purposes will be actualized may be assured. But *how* and *by whom* God's purpose will be realized is not at all clear. God's purpose may be hindered, rejected, misunderstood, as well as discerned, embraced, and served. The presence of such real options in the Lukan account raises the dramatic quality of the narrative while at the same time raising the stakes on readers' responses to the purpose of God.

Foremost among the explicit records of contrasting aims is Luke 7:29–30. Although it is not altogether clear to whom this report should be attributed – Jesus' continued interpretation of the significance of John's mission or Luke's parenthetical aside to the reader? – the primary point is transparent enough. "The people," including toll-collectors, are contrasted with Pharisees and lawyers. The former accepted John's repentance-baptism, signifying their fundamental life-orientation around the way of the Lord and their commitment to live faithfully as children of Abraham (cf. 3:3–14); the latter refused John's baptism, and thus rejected God's purpose (βουλή), showing themselves by their lives to be not children of Abraham but the offspring of poisonous snakes (cf. 3:7–9).

The story of Jesus' passion and death (Luke 22–23) emphasizes competing aims as well. Pilate desired (θέλω) to release Jesus, but finally gave Jesus over to the will (θέλημα) of the chief priests, leaders, and people in Jerusalem (23:20, 25, 13).

---

[8] Siegfried Schulz, "Gottes Vorsehung bei Lukas," *ZNW* 54 (1963) 104–16; cf. the indictment of Lukan interests by Ernst Haenchen (*The Acts of the Apostles: A Commentary* [Oxford: Basil Blackwell, 1971] with reference to Acts 10:1–11:18): "Here stands revealed a peculiarity of Lucan theology which can scarcely be claimed as a point in its favour: in endeavoring to make the hand of God visible in the history of the Church, Luke virtually excludes all human decision" (362).

Joseph, on the other hand, a good and righteous man, had not been party to the purpose (βουλή) of the Jewish Council (23:50–51). With this juxtaposition of aims, the stage is set for the contrast-formula that will appear as a litany in the mission sermons of Acts. For example: "You denied the holy and righteous one and requested that a murderer be given to you; you killed the author life, whom God raised from the dead" (Acts 3:14–15).[9]

Jesus himself can be tested in his resolve to act as God's Son – that is, to act with unreserved obedience to God's will – and can experience in his own life the presence of competing aims. Immediately following his baptism, he was led by the Spirit into the wilderness where he was tested by the devil (4:1–13). In Israel's Scriptures and subsequent Jewish tradition, fidelity to God was proven in the midst of testing, sometimes via the direct activity of the devil.[10] Here, diabolic testing seeks specifically to controvert Jesus' role as Son of God. First, Jesus is encouraged to assert his independence from God (4:1–4). Second, the devil invites Jesus to take his place as the devil's son – that is, to give the devil his allegiance and service (4:5–8). Finally, Jesus is urged to act as though he were obeying God while in fact denying God's purpose and, by extrapolation, serving the purpose of the devil (4:9–12). With varying degrees of deceit, then, the devil strikes at the heart of what it means for Jesus to be "Son of God" in the Lukan narrative – namely, the one who would carry out his mission in absolute allegiance to God, serve without compromise God's redemptive purpose, and as God's agent rule his everlasting kingdom. At the other end of the Gospel, we find Jesus in an analogous struggle, this time in prayer to God: "Father, if you are willing (βούλομαι), remove this cup from me." Jesus is concerned *to discern* God's will and, having discerned it, to *do* it: "nevertheless, not my will (θέλημα) but yours be done" (22:42).

---

[9] On the contrast-formula in Acts, see Jürgen Roloff, "Anfänge der soteriologischen Deutung des Todes Jesu," *NTS* 19 (1972–73) 38–64.

[10] Cf., e.g., Gen. 3:1–19; 22:1–19; Exod. 15:25–26; Job; *2 Apoc. Bar.* 79:2; CD 1:15; 1QS 3:24; 5:4–5; See Heinrich Seesemann, "πεῖρα κτλ.," *TDNT* 6:23–36 (25–27); Graham H. Twelftree, "Temptation of Jesus," in *DJG*, 821–7 (821); Birger

The purpose of God, then, may be countered or opposed in a host of ways within the Gospel, and by a plurality of characters. The juxtaposition of the Roman census in Luke 2:1–7 (mentioned 4 times in the space of 7 verses) with the coming of Jesus, together with the giving of titles to Jesus used elsewhere in Luke's world for the emperor (e.g., "Savior" and "Lord" – cf. Luke 2:1, 11), emphasizes the opposition of Jesus' arrival to the status quo of the Roman empire. Demonic forces are at work throughout the Gospel, too. The well-defined and active hand of the devil or Satan may be present only in a few instances (Luke 4:1–13; 22:3), but Jesus can describe the whole of his public ministry as having been conducted in the midst of diabolic opposition (ἐν τοῖς πειρασμοῖς μου ["in my testings"] – 22:28; cf. 4:13; 8:13).[11] And, according to Jesus' own testimony, the presence of the eschatological kingdom through his ministry is exhibited by the casting out of demons (11:20). Indeed, it is not too much to say that Luke regards any aim that opposes that of God as diabolically motivated.[12] As a consequence, when he is encountered on the Mount of Olives by a posse from the Jewish leadership and temple authorities, Jesus interprets their activity as the extension of "the power of darkness" (22:53; cf. Acts 26:18, where "darkness" is likened to "satanic rule").

The certainty of God's purpose

Recognition of competing aims should not blind us to what for Luke is a central, apologetic emphasis – namely, *the certainty that God's aim will be accomplished*. Initial disbelief (1:20), war and revolution (21:9), even the death of God's Son (9:22; 17:25; *et al.*) cannot derail the plan of God. At the same time that Jesus

Gerhardsson, *The Testing of God's Son (Matt 4:1–11 & par): An Analysis of an Early Christian Midrash*, ConBNT 2 (Lund: Gleerup, 1966) 27–28, 31–35.

11 Numerous questions have been raised against Hans Conzelmann's allegation of a "Satan-free period," stretching from 4:13 to 22:3 (*Theology of St. Luke* [London: Faber and Faber, 1960] e.g. 156–57); cf. most recently Joseph A. Fitzmyer, *Luke the Theologian: Aspects of His Teaching* (New York/Mahwah: Paulist, 1989) ch. 6.

12 Cf. Susan R. Garrett, *The Demise of the Devil: Magic and the Demonic in Luke's Writings* (Minneapolis: Fortress, 1989).

God's design

35

anticipates his suffering and death, he is also anticipating divine rescue through death and participation in the coming banquet of God's kingdom (22:15–18). Of particular interest in Luke's account is the interpretation of Jesus' death as the fulfillment of God's redemptive purpose.[13] As has often been remarked,[14] Luke seems more concerned to emphasize *that* the cross served the divine aim rather than to explicate *how* it thus serves. The heinous death of Jesus was no surprise to God, no obstacle to God's purpose – this is a fundamental affirmation for Luke. It is grounded in Scripture (e.g., 24:45–46) and even in Jesus' own prophetic word (24:6–7). Hostility to Jesus (and by extension, to God's plan) is even capable of being employed in the service of the will of God. Followers of Jesus faced with questions about the enigma of the cross or bewildered by the nature of his demise may find here confirmation of their faith.

Invitation to response

Although the presence of competing aims cannot for Luke negate the unveiling of God's purpose in its fullness, it does have an important function within the narrative. *It is an important means by which persons are confronted with the invitation to align themselves with God's purpose.* Luke's verb of divine necessity, δεῖ, can be used to outline and call for proper response to God. For example, some Pharisees are told that "it was necessary" not only that they tithe (which they are in the habit of doing) but also that they practice justice and love. Instead of the latter, though, they have been distancing themselves from those in need of justice on account of their own status-seeking agenda (11:42–44). Similarly, when the Parable of the Lost Son (15:11–32) is read within its larger narrative co-text, the father's final words to his elder son take on expanded meaning. His observation, "it was necessary that we celebrate and rejoice," is also directed at those Pharisees and scribes who

---

[13] Cf. Gerhard Schneider, *Verleugnung, Verspottung und Verhör Jesu nach Lukas 22,54–71: Studien zur lukanischen Darstellung der Passion*, SANT 22 (Munich: Kösel, 1969) 174–81.
[14] See below, pp. 64–68.

grumble when Jesus plays host to celebrative meals with toll-collectors and sinners (15:1–2). This, it appears, is the appropriate response to the salvific activity of God among the outcasts of society (15:6, 9, 23–24); how will the Pharisees and scribes respond? How will we?

In addition, Luke provides narrative pictures of people who respond favorably to the will of God. Following the announcement to Mary of the birth of God's Son (1:26–38), Mary replies to God's messenger, "Here am I, the servant of the Lord. Let it be with me according to your word." She unreservedly embraces the purpose of God, without regard to its personal cost to her. Moreover, in describing herself as the Lord's servant (cf. 1:48), she both acknowledges her submission to God's purpose and her role in assisting that purpose, and also claims a place in God's household. That is, her response is one of absolute identification with God and his aims so that partnership in the purpose of God transcends even the claims of family (cf. 8:19–21; 9:57–62; 12:51–53; 14:25–26; 18:28–30).

A further example to which we have already alluded is in the material on John the Baptist in Luke 3. Luke underscores John's message of repentance (3:3, 8), an emphasis that signals John's understanding that the status quo has been found wanting. His message thus constitutes a prophetic appeal for people to turn their backs on previous loyalties and commitments and align themselves fundamentally with God's purpose. That the ministry of John is purposely set within the framework of and over against the political leaders of his day (including both Roman and Jewish leaders, 3:1–6), presents people with the option of choosing between those who rule from the urban centers of the Roman world, and him to whom the word of God has come in the wilderness.

John's baptism serves as an appropriate sign of this choice since it asks of people that they come away from normal existence, undergo a repentance-baptism signifying their (re)new(ed) allegiance to God's purpose, then return to their normal lives having accepted the challenge to reflect in their lives ways of living appropriate to true children of Abraham. John's proclamation ensures that his baptism is understood as an assault on the status quo, that to participate in his baptism is to embrace behavior rooted in a radical realignment with God's purpose. John's subsequent ethical message contains within it a social critique that both points the finger of judgment at large-scale injustice and reaches into the realities of day-to-day existence (3:7–14). Life at the local level and one's own normal network of relationships are touched by this ethical vision, with the result that repentance (i.e., aligning oneself around God's purpose) must be understood within and acted out at even the most mundane levels.

GOD, ANGELS, AND THE HOLY SPIRIT

Although in his reflection on the nature of character-building Aristotle privileged *action* over the *actor* (*Poetics* 6.7–21 §§1449b–1450b), it is apparent that the reader of Luke's narrative can make no such easy distinction. With respect to Luke's understanding of God, Luke can bring to the fore a litany of divine activity (e.g., 1:46–55, 68–79; cf. Acts 13:17–25), but these are set in interpretive relation with his identity as "God my Savior" (1:47) and his covenant faithfulness to his old promises (1:54–55, 70, 73; cf. Acts 13:32–33). God rarely enters the narrative of the Third Gospel as a character, and then he does so only indirectly by means of his voice (3:22; 9:35). Nevertheless, references to God abound ("God" [θεός] appears in the Third Gospel 122 times) and throughout the narrative there are evidences that God is the one guiding the events with which Luke is concerned. As we have seen, Luke regularly draws attention to the presence of God in the background of the story. He does this by means of references to God's purpose, the divine purpose that gives rise to the story of Jesus and pushes it to its climax in Jesus' exaltation and beyond. In addition, God is seen to be at work through the lives of others in the story. That is, in accomplishing his aim

God employs the assistance of a series of "helpers."[15] Among these, Jesus is obviously the most important for Luke. As God's Son, Jesus so identifies with God's purpose that to welcome Jesus is to welcome God who sent him (cf. 9:48). Indeed, Jesus asserts,

All things have been handed over to me by my Father; and no one knows who the Son is except the Father, or who the Father is except the Son and anyone to whom the Son chooses to reveal him. (10:22)

Discussion of Luke's presentation of Jesus will be delayed until chapter 3. At present we may focus on other expressions of God's hand in the story of Jesus as Luke narrates it. These include helpers of a supernatural kind – especially the Holy Spirit and angels, but also other affirmations of God's redemptive coming and evidence of the divine choreography of events.

The handiwork of God

From the very outset, the events Luke will narrate are set within the interpretive framework of *God's gracious intervention in history*. Zechariah blesses God, "for he has looked favorably on his people and redeemed them" (1:68). "Looking with favor" is an expression used elsewhere in Luke to point to God's gracious coming (ἐπισκέπτομαι ["to visit"] – 1:68, 78; 7:16; ἐπισκοπή ["visitation"] – 19:44), repeatedly within narrative settings emphasizing the redemptive ministry of Jesus. Using different language, Simeon witnesses to a similar understanding of Jesus' coming. Addressing God with the rare appellation "Master" (δεσπότης – 2:29), he recognizes God's fingerprints in the activity surrounding Jesus. The coming of Jesus is the coming of salvation, in continuity with prophetic anticipation (2:29–32; cf. Isa. 49:6).

Mention of Simeon highlights a further manifestation of divine handiwork beneath the surface of the narrative. The

---

15 Noting that "the [narrative] aim is difficult to achieve," Bal observes that, within the narrative, "the subject meets with resistance on the way and receives help" (*Narratology*, 30). "Helpers," then, are those who form "a necessary but in itself insufficient condition to reach the aim" (31).

whole encounter between Mary, Joseph, and Jesus on the one hand and Simeon on the other is carefully – one might say, divinely – choreographed. Mary and Joseph bring Jesus to the temple "according to the law of Moses" (2:22), "as it is written in the law of the Lord" (2:23), "according to what is stated in the law of the Lord" (2:24), according to "what was customary under the law" (2:27), in obedience to the "law of the Lord" (2:39). Meanwhile, Simeon, "on whom the Holy Spirit rested" (2:25), was "guided by the Spirit" (2:27) into the temple. In this account, God's ancient law and the Holy Spirit work in tandem to bring these two parties together for a programmatic and revelatory moment, a divine encounter (2:25–35). This is not an occasion for Luke to teach that "law" is now superseded by "Spirit";[16] rather, it demonstrates the continuity of faithfulness to the Scriptures and guidance of the Spirit in God's one salvific purpose.

Miracles also evidence the activity of God within the Lukan narrative to further his redemptive purpose. This is most obvious in summary passages in Acts, where in retrospect the signs and wonders performed by Jesus are credited to God's working through Jesus (Acts 2:22; cf. 14:3), or to Jesus' "doing good and healing" as a consequence of his having been anointed by God (10:38). But this emphasis is already transparent in the Gospel. Thus, all that Jesus does throughout his public ministry follows from and grows out of his having been empowered by the Holy Spirit (cf. 4:1, 14–15, 18–19). Moreover, in the Third Gospel Jesus' healing activity repeatedly results in people giving praise *to God* (cf., e.g., 5:25–26; 7:16; *et al.*). In Jesus' ministry of healing, the people recognize the activity of God.[17]

---

[16] *Contra* René Laurentin, *The Truth of Christmas: Beyond the Myths. The Gospels of the Infancy of Christ*, SS (Petersham, Massachusetts: St. Bede's, 1986).

[17] Cf. Paul J. Achtemeier, "The Lukan Perspective on the Miracles of Jesus: A Preliminary Sketch," in *Perspectives on Luke– Acts*, ed. Charles H. Talbert (Danville, Virginia: Association of Baptist Professors of Religion; Edinburgh: T. & T. Clark, 1978) 153–67 (158–59) (and the added nuance in Robert Tannehill, *The Narrative Unity of Luke–Acts: A Literary Interpretation*, vol. 1 (Philadelphia, Fortress), 86–87, where it is noted that the faith to which miracles lead is faith *in God*); Larry W. Hurtado, "God," in *DJG*, 270–76 (274).

Angels

The aim of God is furthered in the Lukan narrative by the presence and activity of angels. During the latter years of the Second Temple period, increased speculation on the nature of the heavenly world and its inhabitants gave rise in some Jewish circles to a highly developed angelology.[18] Particularly with reference to an "angel of the Lord" and the identification of this angel as "Gabriel" (e.g., 1:11–20), Luke may be drawing on those developments (but cf. already, e.g., Exod. 14:19; Judg. 13:3–5; Daniel 8–9; Zech. 1:11–14). In any case, it is manifest that Luke's narrative is not itself concerned with an angelology *per se*, but presents angels only in their subordinate role as those who serve the divine project.

As in the OT, "the angel of the Lord" is presented in Luke 1–2 as a special agent of God, who helps God to accomplish his will (cf. Exod. 3:2; Judg. 6:11–16). In particular, this divine servant serves as a surrogate for the presence of God (in the Holy Place, 1:11) and so as God's mouthpiece: communicating God's favor (1:28, 30) and judgment (1:20); and announcing the births of John and Jesus, together with their redemptive significance (1:13–20, 30–38; 2:9–12). In this role, Gabriel's words are set alongside the words of Scripture as expressions of the divine purpose. Moreover, Gabriel himself interprets the Scriptures to Zechariah and Mary, drawing especially on the Elijah-tradition with respect to John (1:14–17; cf. Mal. 4:5–6; Sir. 48:1–12) and the David-tradition with respect to Jesus (1:32–33; cf., e.g., 2 Sam. 7:12–16). Angels are also present at the empty tomb, where they remind the first witnesses of the resurrection, faithful women from Galilee, of Jesus' words concerning his death and resurrection (24:1–7). Interestingly, within the Lukan accounts of the empty tomb and resurrection appearances (i.e., Luke 24), angels again serve in tandem with Scripture as conveyers of God's redemptive purpose.

Angels also appear as members of the heavenly entourage

---

[18] See the brief summary in Carol Newsom and Duane F. Watson, "Angels," in *ABD*, 1:251–53.

(9:26; 12:8–9), who rejoice at the repentance of sinners (15:10) and act on behalf of a beggar so poor he does not even receive burial (16:22). And they assist Jesus as he struggles on the Mount of Olives to discern and submit to the will of the Father (22:43–44).[19] Little wonder, then, that Jesus remarks that "children of the resurrection" are "like angels" (20:34–36) – not only because they do not die (as in 20:36), but because they, like the angels of Luke's Gospel, embody the divine purpose.

The Holy Spirit

Even more central to Luke's narrative theology is the Holy Spirit. This is especially true of Luke's second volume, the Acts of the Apostles, but the prominence of the Spirit there is foreshadowed by the Spirit's presence already in volume one, the Gospel of Luke. It is by means of the presence and activity of the Holy Spirit that Luke establishes the continuity of God's one salvific purpose.

In the Third Gospel, the Holy Spirit is actively engaged in two primary and closely related ways that extend the purpose of God. First, it is through the Spirit that God's purpose is announced and celebrated, above all in the birth narratives of Luke 1–2. Second, the Spirit enables the service and fulfillment of God's plan.

In the opening chapters of Luke, the births of John and Jesus are celebrated and interpreted by those who are filled with the Holy Spirit. It is said specifically of Elizabeth that upon hearing Mary's greeting, she "was filled with the Holy Spirit and exclaimed with a loud cry, 'Blessed are you among women ...'" (1:41–42). Similarly, Zechariah, once he receives his voice, "was filled with the Holy Spirit and prophesied" (1:67). Simeon is characterized as a prophet on whom the Holy Spirit rested (2:25). Anna is a "prophet," and so speaks as enabled by the Spirit (2:36–38). Among those who speak of

---

[19] Some mss. and some modern translations (e.g., RSV) omit these verses; for their originality see Joel B. Green, "Jesus on the Mount of Olives (Luke 22:39–46): Tradition and Theology," *JSNT* 26 (1986) 29–48 (35–36).

God's activity in the events of the birth narratives, Mary alone is not explicitly so characterized.[20] On closer examination, however, she seems less an exception, for Gabriel proclaims to her, "The Holy Spirit will come upon you, and the power of the Most High will overshadow you" (1:35). Although the immediate purpose of this activity of the Spirit relates to the conception and bearing of a son, to be named Jesus, the parallels with Acts 1:8 are unmistakable. The Song of Mary (1:46–55), then, may be understood also as the utterance of a Spirit-filled person.[21]

On the one hand, this points to the important degree to which the Holy Spirit's role in Luke is related to divine empowerment to speak. On the other, this enabling presence of the Spirit makes of women and men persons who are able to understand and proclaim the divine purpose, especially its fulfillment in God's intervention in the coming of Jesus. And they do so with profound images of divine deliverance rooted in the covenantal graciousness of God. Importantly, within the narrative, the words of Mary and Elizabeth, Simeon and Zechariah are for *our ears*. None of these characters appear again during the public ministries of John and Jesus. They are given no opportunity within the story of Jesus as Luke relates it to communicate this important news to characters within the narrative (like Peter or Martha or the Jewish leadership).

Three corollaries grow out of these observations. First, speaking as persons empowered by the Spirit, Simeon, Elizabeth, and the others are presented as spokespersons for God. What they say of John, Jesus, and the character of God's salvation brings with it the divine imprimatur.[22] Second, we

---

[20] It is for this reason that some find attractive the alternative ascription of the Magnificat to Elizabeth (read in: it[a,b,l]* Ir[lat] Or[lat.mss]). Elizabeth, not Mary, is explicitly described as having been filled with the Spirit (cf. the potential parallel in 1:67–79). But the case against this attribution is overwhelming – cf. Paul Bemile, *The Magnificat within the Context and Framework of Lukan Theology: An Exegetical, Theological Study of Lk 1:46–55*, RST 34 (Frankfurt-on-Main: Peter Lang, 1986) 5–19.

[21] Cf. James B. Shelton, *Mighty in Word and Deed: The Role of the Holy Spirit in Luke–Acts* (Peabody, Massachusetts: Hendrickson, 1991) 20–21.

[22] *Contra* J. Massyngbaerde Ford, *My Enemy Is My Guest: Jesus and Violence in Luke* (Maryknoll, New York: Orbis, 1984), who argues that Luke 1–2 establish violent

may take as thoroughly reliable the characterization of John and Jesus, as well as of God and God's redemptive activity, outlined in their Spirit-inspired words. For example, because deliverance-as-social-transformation and as reconciliation with God are emphasized in these prophetic words, we may with good reason read the rest of the Gospel of Luke looking for the outworking of these visions of salvation. Third, we must realize that we, as readers, have a kind of "inside intelligence." This means not only that we know more than the characters within the Gospel narrative, but also (and therefore) that we, as readers, are given a responsibility to discern, respond to, and embrace God's purpose that is concomitant with this greater understanding. Put another way, Luke presents the Holy Spirit as acting *through the narrative* to encourage understanding and response on the part of Luke's audience.

The Holy Spirit also empowers persons to serve God's purpose. This is evident immediately in the description of John the Baptist. According to the angel Gabriel, even before John is born he will be filled with the Spirit (1:15). Thus empowered, he is able, from the womb, to begin his prophetic ministry (1:41, 44). Luke's later portrait of John continues this theme (cf. 3:2–6).

The other person in the Third Gospel who is said to be filled with the Spirit and whose activity is guided and empowered by the Spirit is, of course, Jesus. In fact, Jesus' operation under the anointing of the Spirit is one of the chief ways Luke presents Jesus, both in the Gospel and, in retrospect, in Acts. The relationship between Jesus and the Spirit in the Gospel of Luke can be explored under three related headings.

First, the conception of Jesus is attributed to the Spirit. Luke 1:32–35 underscores the eschatological role of the Holy Spirit by relating the Spirit's work to the conception of the eschatolo-

---

images of salvation that will be overturned in Luke 3–24. What we have observed certifies that the images of salvation in Luke 1–2, while susceptible to further definition or nuance, are not for Luke "wrong." This observation also speaks against the thesis of Robert A. Tannehill ("Israel in Luke–Acts: A Tragic Story," *JBL* 104 [1985] 69–85), that Luke raises expectations for Israel's salvation through Jesus in Luke 1–2 which go unfulfilled in the narrative as a whole; see further below, pp. 98–99.

gical Son of God who will occupy the throne of David into perpetuity. Born as a result of the intervention of the Spirit, Jesus will be holy. As Gerhard Schneider comments, "Jesus is not only *filled* with the Spirit like John is (1:15); rather, he owes his very *being (Existenz)* to the Spirit of God."[23]

Second, Jesus' public ministry grows out of his experience of the Spirit. The baptism of Jesus is portrayed by Luke in such a way so as to minimize emphasis either on the work of John or on the baptism itself (2:21–22). In fact, in a characteristically Lukan fashion, before Jesus comes on the scene in order to be baptized, John has been removed from center stage – arrested and shut up in prison by Herod (2:18–20). The event of baptism itself is described as little more than the time during which something else happened, something of far greater importance – namely, "the heaven was opened, and the Holy Spirit descended upon [Jesus]" (3:21–22). This is followed by a divine affirmation of Jesus' status and identity as Son of God (3:22).

The importance of this Spirit-anointing and presentation of Jesus as Son of God is paramount in the developing narrative. Luke immediately confirms Jesus' status by an alternative route, by providing for Jesus a genealogy that traces Jesus' lineage back to "Adam, son of God" (3:23–28). Subsequently, Jesus, "full of the Holy Spirit, returned from the Jordan and was led by the Spirit in the wilderness" to be tested, following which "Jesus returned to Galilee in the power of the Spirit" (4:1, 14). Then, in 4:18, citing Isa. 61:1, Jesus announces, "The Spirit of the Lord is upon me, because he has anointed me." The importance of this portrayal is then underscored in Acts 10:38, where Peter speaks of "how God anointed Jesus of Nazareth with the Holy Spirit and with power; how he went about doing good and healing all who were under the power of the devil, for God was with him." Elsewhere in the Third Gospel, Jesus is not regularly presented in an explicit way as carrying on his work under the empowerment of the Spirit

---

[23] Gerhard Schneider, *Das Evangelium nach Lukas*, vol. 1, 2nd. ed., OTKNT 3.1 (Gütersloh: Gerd Mohn; Würtzburg: Echter, 1984) 53.

(though cf. 10:21–24). This should not blind us, however, to the importance of these affirmations concerning Jesus. Remembering that Luke is writing a *narrative account* of Jesus' ministry, the profound emphasis he places on the Spirit's empowerment and guidance of Jesus at the outset of his narrative demonstrates that the whole of Jesus' public ministry is Spirit-empowered. And this is confirmed by the retrospective summary in Acts 10:38. Moreover, when Luke encapsulates the content of the Gospel in Acts 1:1–3, he attributes the whole of Jesus' ministry to his agency as the Spirit-endowed representative of God. That is, throughout the whole of his ministry, Jesus operates in the sphere of the Spirit and his power is derived from the Spirit. Thus, the Spirit's activity with regard to Jesus is integral to his birth, identity, and mission as Son of God.

What role does Luke attribute to the Spirit? Some studies have attempted to present too narrow an understanding of the place of the Spirit in Luke's theology, asserting that Luke thinks only of the activity of the Spirit in empowering witness or prophetic speech.[24] In part, this has resulted from perceptions that Second Temple Judaism limited the role of the Spirit narrowly, thinking only of "the spirit of prophecy." Further study has broadened the catalog of the functions of the Spirit in Judaism, however, extending it to include a creative function and as the power behind the working of miraculous deeds.[25] That the empowering of the Spirit is related not only to inspired speech but also to miraculous activity is manifest within the narrative of Luke, not least in the programmatic announcement of Jesus at Nazareth (4:18–19). There, Jesus' mission is cast in terms encompassing a range of activity: proclamation, healing, releasing the oppressed. When it is

---

[24] For this view, see most recently, e.g., Shelton, *Mighty in Word and Deed*; Robert P. Menzies, *The Development of Early Christian Pneumatology: With Special Reference to Luke–Acts*, JSNTSS 54 (Sheffield: JSOT, 1991). See the important critique of this view in Max Turner, "The Spirit and the Power of Jesus' Miracles in the Lucan Conception," *NovT* 33 (1991) 124–52.

[25] See Max Turner, "Holy Spirit," in *DJG*, 341–51 (342); cf. Max Turner "The Spirit of Prophecy and of Authoritative Preaching in Luke–Acts: A Question of Origins," *NTS* 38 (1992) 66–88.

considered that "releasing the oppressed" relates in Luke–Acts
to "release from sins and their consequences in the community
of God's people" as well as "release for those under the power
of the devil, including those whose illness is an expression of
diabolic oppression,"[26] then the activity for which Jesus was
anointed is easily expanded to include the totality of his ministry as narrated in the Third Gospel.

The Spirit is active in the conception of Jesus, but is also
experienced as the guide and empowerment behind the whole
of his mission. Third, the work of the Spirit within and among
the followers of Jesus, so central in Acts, is anticipated with
reference to Jesus' ministry in Luke.

Already John had promised that Jesus, as Messiah, would
"baptize you with the Holy Spirit and with fire" (3:16). Jesus
himself furthers this expectation in 11:13: "How much more
will the heavenly Father give the Holy Spirit to those who ask
him!" Moreover, in his final instructions before his ascension as
reported in Luke 24:49, Jesus refers to "what my Father
promised" – namely, the gift of the Holy Spirit (cf. 11:13; Acts
1:4–5). To this data we may add 12:12, where Jesus promises
the help of the Holy Spirit to those brought before hostile
political and religious leaders. In all of these instances, we see
how what was true of Jesus, that he carried on his ministry in
the sphere of the Spirit while deriving his power from the
Spirit, will also be true of his followers. Jesus in fact says as
much during his post-resurrection ministry with the apostles:
"Rather, you will receive power when the Holy Spirit comes
upon you, and you will be my witnesses in Jerusalem, in all
Judea and Samaria, and to the end of the earth" (Acts 1:8);
and this is the experience of the community of Jesus' followers
following Pentecost. For them, as well as for him, the Spirit is
the enabling presence of God to discern, embrace, and serve

---

[26] Cf. Luke 13:10–17; Acts 10:38; Joel B. Green, "'Proclaiming Repentance and
Forgiveness of Sins to All Nations': A Biblical Perspective on the Church's
Mission," in *The World Is My Parish: The Mission of the Church in Methodist Perspective*,
ed. Alan G. Padgett, SHM 10 (Lewiston, New York: Edwin Mellen, 1992) 13–43
(24–34).

the redemptive purpose of God. The Holy Spirit is the power that puts into effect the will of God.[27]

THE PURPOSE OF GOD AND LUKE–ACTS

At least three important repercussions grow out of this discussion of the centrality of God's purpose to Lukan thought. First, this becomes an important witness for the fundamental theological *and* narratological unity of Luke's two volumes, Luke and Acts. Luke's agenda is not to write the story of Jesus, followed by the story of the early church (or of a few representative apostles and missionaries). Rather, his design is to write the story of the continuation and fulfillment of God's project – a story that embraces both the work of Jesus and of the followers of Jesus after his ascension. From start to finish, Luke–Acts brings to the fore one narrative aim, the one aim of God.

In narrative terms, one can think of the development of the Lukan material following a path from anticipation to possibility to probability to realization to results. Painted in these broad strokes, we see the working out of God's purpose to bring salvation to all people. This aim is *anticipated* by voices of angels and Spirit-inspired persons in Luke 1:5–2:52. It is made possible by the birth and growth of John and Jesus in households that honor God. But this is not an aim that will be reached easily or without opposition. It requires the positive response of people like Mary and others, for God's aim necessarily involves the collusion of human actors. The realization of God's aim is made *probable* through the ministries of John and Jesus (including Jesus' life, death, and exaltation) and by the consequent commissioning and promised empowering of Jesus' followers (Luke 3 – Acts 1). Of course, Jesus himself prepares the way for this universal mission, not by engaging much with non-Jews, but by repeatedly calling into question those barriers that divide ethnic groups, men and women, adults and children,

---

[27] Cf. Hans von Baer, *Der heilige Geist in den Lukasschriften* (Stuttgart: Kohlhammer, 1926).

rich and poor, righteous and sinner, and so on. Acts, then, narrates the *realization* of God's purpose, particularly in Acts 2–15, as the Christian mission is directed by God to take the necessary steps to achieve an egalitarian community composed of Jews, Samaritans, and Gentiles. The *results* of this narrative aim (Acts 16–28) highlight more and more Jewish antagonism to the Christian movement, and the church appears more and more to be Gentile in make-up. But even this is God's purpose, and efforts among the Jewish people at interpreting Moses and the prophets as showing the Messiah is Jesus should continue.[28]

In short, the Gospel of Luke creates needs related to God's purpose that go unfulfilled in Luke, but are addressed directly in Acts. And this draws attention to the unity of Luke and Acts at the narrative level.[29]

Second, the importance Luke gives to the divine purpose in his narration has implications for our understanding of the genre of his work. In chapter 1 we pointed to reasons for taking Luke and Acts together as historiography. John Squires has examined Luke's concern with the plan of God against the background of providence in Hellenistic historiography.[30] His work not only provides further reason to believe the author of Luke–Acts worked with historiographical purposes in mind. It also indicates the importance of this recognition for showing how Luke's work might have been read – as a confirmation of their faith, well rooted as it is in God's own purpose and activity, and as an attempt already to translate the gospel in a way tailored to a world concerned at least in part with popular philosophical ideas related to the role of the divine in human affairs.

Finally, Luke's unrelenting emphasis on the purpose of God is presented as an invitation. People *within* the narrative may

---

28 This summary of the aim of Luke–Acts borrows heavily on Green, "Problem of a Beginning."

29 For a contrary view, see Mikeal C. Parsons and Richard I. Pervo, *Rethinking the Unity of Luke and Acts* (Minneapolis: Fortress, 1993). My forthcoming commentaries on the Gospel of Luke (NICNT; Grand Rapids, Michigan: Wm. B. Eerdmans) and the Acts of the Apostles (WBC; Dallas, Texas: Word) will develop this unity in detail.

30 Squires, *Plan of God*.

embrace or reject the divine aim. Luke's readers receive the same invitation. They are encouraged to listen carefully to the Scriptures of Israel, to follow the course of the ministry of Jesus, and so to adopt a perspective internal to the narrative itself. Having done so, Luke's readers may hear the challenge of Jesus to side with those who side with God's redemptive project, and having done so to serve it as those empowered by the Holy Spirit. This is the call of discipleship in Luke: to align oneself with Jesus, who aligns himself fundamentally and absolutely with God.

CHAPTER 3

"A Savior, who is the Messiah, the Lord": Jesus, John, and the Jewish people

For Luke–Acts, the controlling aim is that of God. But the central character within the Gospel narrative is Jesus of Nazareth, whose prominence is a function both of his commitment to God's purpose and of his status as the one through whom that purpose is articulated and realized. As the Song of Mary has it, even the news of the imminent birth of Jesus is enough to secure the affirmation that God's salvation has already begun (1:46–55).[1]

This identification of Jesus with God's purpose is not unexpected in a Gospel that highlights so pervasively Jesus' status and role as Son of God. Although Luke was free to develop this appellation in his own way within the narrative, the term "son" (υἱός) as it circulated in antiquity would already have suggested certain nuances.[2] These included the son's obedience to his father, the father's role as primary educator of his son, and the son's service as his father's agent, his surrogate. In fact, Luke builds his perspective on Jesus on the foundation of these ways of understanding sonship. For him, Jesus' role as God's Son was characterized by his allegiance to God's purpose and his service as God's envoy.

---

[1] The verbs used to designate God's activity in 1:51–54 appear in the aorist tense, referring, as I. Howard Marshall puts it, to events "which had already begun to take place at the time of the hymn" (*The Gospel of Luke: A Commentary on the Greek Text*, NIGTC [Grand Rapids, Michigan: Wm. B. Eerdmans; Exeter: Paternoster, 1978] 84).

[2] See A. E. Harvey, *Jesus and the Constraints of History* (Philadelphia: Westminster, 1982) 154–73; James D. G. Dunn, *Christology in the Making: A New Testament Inquiry into the Origins of the Doctrine of the Incarnation* (Philadelphia: Westminster, 1980) 13–22.

JOHN AND JESUS: FIRST APPEARANCES

Beginnings are important, and the first two chapters of the Third Gospel begin already Luke's agenda of defining the significance of Jesus. He does this in at least two ways: first, by the way he has structured the birth narratives; second, by his focus on the status of Jesus as God's Son.

John and Jesus in parallel

The dominant feature on the terrain of Luke 1–2 is the parallelism between John and Jesus. Most obvious here is the juxtaposition of the annunciation episodes (1:5–23, 26–38) and the accounts of birth-circumcision-naming (1:57–66; 2:1–27, 34–39). The parallels are much more extensive, however, and, in fact, embrace the whole of Luke 1:5–2:52:[3]

The introduction of parents (1:5–7, 26–27)
Luke prefaces both annunciation accounts with an introduction of the parents-to-be. Both begin with chronological markers, followed by the introduction of the males and females in parallel formulae. Considerable attention is devoted to issues of status – with Zechariah and Elizabeth noted for their priestly lineage, advanced age (in a culture where honor comes with age), and exemplary piety. Joseph, too, has an enviable birthright, though Mary is young and no reference is made to her family. Finally, both introductions dwell on issues of childbearing status.

The Annunciation (1:8–23, 28–38)
Both accounts name Gabriel as God's messenger. In form the two stories are parallel and also bear resemblances to other

---

[3] This parallelism has been noted often, though no one has argued that all of the material in Luke 1:5–2:52 may be understood as fitting into a parallel scheme. Cf. Raymond E. Brown, *The Birth of the Messiah: A Commentary on the Infancy Narratives in Matthew and Luke* (Garden City, New York: Doubleday, 1977) 250–53; Stephen Farris, *The Hymns of Luke's Infancy Narratives: Their Origin, Meaning and Significance*, JSNTSS 9 (Sheffield: JSOT, 1985) 99–107.

biblical stories of birth announcement and commission.[4] Both
Zechariah and Mary are promised sons through extraordinary
circumstances, both are given names for their sons and
informed of their missions, and with regard to both, the activity
of the Holy Spirit is promised. Zechariah and Mary each
address a question to Gabriel and are given signs.

The mother's response (1:24–25, 39–56)

Both episodes take place in Elizabeth's home (1:24, 40, 56) and
begin with parallel references to "those days" (1:24, 39).
Elizabeth and Mary each speak of what the Lord "has done for
me" when he looked "on me" with favor. As a result of God's
doing, both women are blessed – Elizabeth's disgrace has been
removed (1:25); and Mary receives a blessing from the Spirit-
filled Elizabeth (1:41, 45).

Because of the earlier parallelism between Mary and Zechariah (above), we might have anticipated a more obvious structural relationship between the Songs of Mary and Zechariah
(1:46–55, 68–79). By now, however, Mary and Elizabeth
occupy the positions of prominence in the narrative, for Zechariah has been silenced. His response of unbelief to the angelic
"good news" (1:19) has delayed his response to the gift of a son
until after John's birth and naming.

The birth (1:57–58; 2:1–20)

Chronological references mark the beginning of both accounts
(1:57; 2:1) and Luke reports the "fulfillment" of the time for
each birth (1:57; 2:6). Both births are set on a public stage –
with Elizabeth's neighbors and relatives introduced in the case
of John's birth (1:58) and shepherds and angels in the case of
Jesus' (2:8–20). Given that Joseph and Mary have gone to the

---

[4] On the annunciation form, cf., e.g., Gen. 16:7–13; 17:1–21; 18:1–15; Judg. 13:3–20;
Matt. 1:20–21; Edgar W. Conrad, "The Annunciation of Birth and the Birth of the
Messiah," *CBQ* 47 (1985) 656–68; Robert Alter, "How Convention Helps Us Read:
The Case of the Bible's Annunciation Type-Scene," *Prooftexts* 3 (1983) 115–30. For
the commission, see, e.g., Exod. 3:1–4:16; Judg. 6:11–24; 1 Kings 19:1–19a; Isaiah 6;
Jer. 1:4–12; Herman Hendrickx, *The Infancy Narratives*, SSG (London: Geoffrey
Chapman, 1984) 57–59; Terence Y. Mullins, "New Testament Commission Forms,
Especially in Luke–Acts," *JBL* 95 (1976) 603–14.

home of Joseph's ancestral family (2:4), the absence of his kin from the story may be surprising, but the account of Jesus' birth is developed so as to emphasize its cosmological import. Responses to both births emphasize God's favor (1:58; 2:14) and joy (1:58; 2:10, 20).

Circumcision and naming (1:59–66; 2:21–24)
The relative length of the story of John's circumcision and naming results from the emphasis on getting the baby's name right, made difficult by Zechariah's inability to speak. The effect is the same, however, as both infants receive the name designated for them by Gabriel (1:13 → 1:59–63; 1:31 → 2:21). The added remarks in 2:22–24 emphasize the blamelessness of Mary and Joseph *vis-à-vis* the law, and are reminiscent of the character references given Zechariah and Elizabeth in 1:6.

Prophetic response (1:67–79; 2:25–39)
After his obedience in the naming of his son, Zechariah is able to speak. Having been filled with the Spirit, he "prophesies" regarding God's redemptive work and the role of his son in the divine purpose (1:67–79). Simeon is portrayed as a prophet and Anna is called a prophet; both announce the role of Jesus in eschatological deliverance.

Growth of the child (1:80; 2:40–52)
John and Jesus are both the subjects of summary comments on their growth.[5] Those concerning Jesus are more complex, since into an *inclusio* marked by the dual summaries in 2:40, 52, Luke has inserted an illustrative story drawing out the nature of Jesus' maturation.[6] At the same time, it is worth noting that 1:80 anticipates John "appearing publicly to Israel," while 2:46–47 anticipates Jesus' later public ministry. Both will have a role in enunciating to Israel the shape of God's purpose.

The presence of such a pervasive parallelism is hardly accidental and invites our viewing these two narrative sequences

---

[5] Cf., e.g., Gen. 20:21; Judg. 13:24–25; Acts 6:7; 9:31.
[6] See the parallel narrative strategy in Acts 6:1a, 1b–6, 7.

together. In fact, these two stories are one, for they demonstrate how God will accomplish his salvific aim.[7] In this regard,
the heavenly and prophetic voices have a signal role, giving
expression to the divine purpose in the progress of the narrative
and inviting reflection and response. The parallel accounts of
promise → fulfillment → response tell one story, the story of
God's intervention in human history to bring deliverance,
consolation, redemption, peace.

The similarities of these two story-lines attract our attention
first. We are struck by the close relationship between these four
parents and their children. Their kinship extends beyond the
ties between Mary and Elizabeth (1:36); their affinity extends
to the centrality of their roles in the one purpose of God.[8] As
the angel affirms, the births of John and Jesus constitute "good
news" (1:19; 2:10).

What of the differences? Clearly, Luke's parallelism is not
one of equals. Repeatedly, the balance is tipped in favor of
Jesus, so that we are left in no doubt as to which is the
preeminent of these two children. Structurally, this is represented by the simple fact that the story of Jesus receives almost
twice as much space in these two chapters as does the story of
John. Two prophetic responses attend Jesus' presentation in
the temple compared to only one in the case of John's naming
and circumcision. And when the two stories converge in
1:39–56, the weight of attention is given to Mary and her
unborn child. We notice that Jesus will be "Son of the Most
High," but John will be "prophet of the Most High" (1:32,
76). It is John who leaps in the womb when Elizabeth and
Mary meet, already testifying to the coming of the Lord
(1:41–44). And so on.

This concern to put John in his place is not surprising in light
of the evidence of Acts. In Acts 13:24–25; 18:25; 19:1–4 we

---

[7] See Charles Thomas Davis III, "The Literary Structure of Luke 1–2," in *Art and Meaning: Rhetoric in Biblical Literature*, ed. David J. A. Clines, David M. Gunn, and Alan J. Hauser, JSOTSS 19 (Sheffield: JSOT, 1982) 215–29.

[8] See Augustin George, "Le Parallèle entre Jean-Baptiste et Jésus en Lc 1–2," in *Mélanges Bibliques en Homage au R. P. Béda Rigaux*, ed. Albert Descamps and R. P. André de Halleux (Gembloux: J. Duculot, 1970) 141–71.

discover the abiding influence of the Baptist movement in a surprisingly wide-reaching geographical sweep, including Asia Minor and Achaia – far from the center of John's activity in the region of the River Jordan. With the living presence of the Baptist circle, no doubt it was important to indicate its relation to the Jesus movement. Without disparaging the eschatological significance of John's ministry, then, Luke communicates in this imbalanced set of parallels the superiority of Jesus.

Jesus: Son of David, Son of God

Turning from an important *structural* feature of the birth narrative, we may also draw attention to the many points of contact with the Davidic material in Luke's presentation of Jesus. First, Joseph is "of the house of David" (1:27); indeed Joseph plays no other role for Luke than to prepare for the identification of his (albeit adopted) son as a Davidid. Second, Jesus' acclamation as Son of God (1:32, 35) must be read at least against the backdrop of the use of this expression to designate the Davidic king in Israel's Scriptures.[9] Third, in 1:32b–33, we hear unmistakable echoes of the divine promise to David of an everlasting dynasty found in 2 Sam. 7:11b–16 – e.g., the reference to David's throne, "his kingdom" (2 Sam. 7:12, 13; cf. v. 16), the perpetual character of this kingdom (2 Sam. 7:13, 16), and the correlation of kingship and sonship (2 Sam. 7:14).

Jesus' sonship also extends to the nature of his conception. The report of the consequence of this divine agency focuses less on virginal conception and more on its christological repercussions. First, Gabriel's words in 1:35 emphasize the relation of the Spirit's activity and Jesus' sonship: Jesus is "Son of God" not as a consequence of his assuming the throne of David (as in Ps. 2:7), but as a result of his conception. Second, though Luke is not working with later trinitarian categories, he is nonetheless moving beyond a functional understanding of Jesus' sonship. Like John, Jesus is set apart (i.e., "holy") from birth to

---

[9] Cf., e.g., 2 Sam. 7:14; 1 Chron. 17:13; 22:10; 28:6; Pss. 2:7; 89:26–27; Jer. 23:5–8; Ezek. 37:21–23; Zech. 3:8–10; 12:17–13:1; Hag. 2:21–22; also, 4 Ezra 12:31–32; *Pss. Sol.* 17–18; 1QM 11:1–18; 4QFlor. 1:11–14; 4QTest. 9–13.

special service in God's redemptive purpose. Jesus' sonship, however, extends backward to the prevenient work of God in his origin as a human being.

Jesus' own awareness of this special relationship with God is then brought to the fore at the end of the birth narrative, in 2:40–52, and especially in 2:48–49. In this account of Jesus' having been left behind in the temple by his parents, Luke has staged the interchange between Jesus and his mother so as to pinpoint the primary issue, who is Jesus' father? To whom does he owe primary allegiance? Jesus' answer to his mother, "Did you not know that I must be in my Father's house?" (NRSV) continues the emphasis of this account on *place* (where Jesus was; where they found him; why would anyone look elsewhere?). However, the issue is not simply a matter of location. Recalling that the notion of "household" in the Greco-Roman milieu was not only a designation of place but also of authority, we may gain a more helpful view of what this scene portends. Jesus is in the temple, the locus of God's presence, and he is there under divine compulsion. The point is that he must align himself with God's purpose, even if this appears to compromise his relationship with Mary and Joseph. This too is what is entailed in his role as "Son of God."

JESUS' EXPERIENCE OF SONSHIP

From baptism to public ministry (3:21–4:30)

The picture of Jesus as Son of God is anticipated in Luke's narrative of the events surrounding Jesus' birth and childhood, then developed further when the adult Jesus is next introduced and begins his public ministry. Luke 3:21–4:30 narrate the preparation and emergence of Jesus to take up his ministry as God's Son.

Previously, we have heard of Jesus' sonship and importance in God's plan via human and angelic voices. In the scene of Jesus' baptism (3:21–22), God himself declares Jesus to be his son, thus providing an unimpeachable sanction for Jesus' identity and mission. That this identification is set in parallel with Jesus' endowment with the Spirit accentuates Jesus' role as God's agent and certifies that Jesus is divinely equipped for his mission.

Following immediately on the heels of Jesus' baptism is a record of his genealogy (3:23–28). This interruption in the unfolding narrative is of significance in the first century, since Jesus and Luke belonged to a social setting where identity and status were determined in large part by one's family heritage.[10] Genealogies serve as indicators of inherited status; hence, it is commonly recognized that these lists might be subject to what anthropologists call "genealogical amnesia" (where problematic ancestors are suppressed) or "idealism" (where lists are adjusted to fulfill new social needs).[11] This helps to explain the discrepancies of Luke's genealogical table *vis-à-vis* that in Matt. 1:1–17 and those in the Old Testament.

How does Luke's genealogy of Jesus function in this co-text? First, Jesus' superiority over John is again emphasized, since John receives no genealogical table. Second, Jesus' genealogy is carefully framed with references to "son of God" in 3:22, 38; together with the repetition of "son of" throughout the list,[12] this allows for a kind of crescendo leading to the acknowledgment of God as the originator of Jesus' line.

Third, at the outset of the genealogy, in an aside to his readership, Luke notes that Jesus "was the son (as was thought) of Joseph" (3:23). By this means, Luke sets up the subsequent problem of Jesus' identity: *we* know that he is God's Son, but others within the narrative have no such "insider knowledge" and will struggle to understand his identity and mission.[13] It is against this background that one should read the response of the synagogue audience in Luke 4:22: believing

---

[10] See Luke's sensitivity to such issues already in the introductions of Zechariah and Elizabeth (1:5), Joseph (1:27; 2:4), and by the use of such expressions as "children of Abraham," "house of David," and "offspring of vipers" (1:55, 69, 73; 3:7–8)

[11] Cf., e.g., Mary Douglas, *How Institutions Think* (Syracuse, New York: Syracuse University Press, 1986) chs. 6–7; Charlotte Seymour-Smith, *Macmillan Dictionary of Anthropology* (London/Basingstoke: Macmillan, 1986) 130.

[12] This is rare in biblical genealogies: cf. 1 Chron. 3:10–24; 6:16–30.

[13] Elsewhere Luke uses νομίζω ("to think," "to assume") to denote an assumption wrongly made that leads persons to act as if it were true – 2:44; Acts 7:25; 8:20; 14:19; 16:27; 21:29.

that Jesus is son of Joseph and, thus, "one of their own," they
assume that the blessings of salvation he announces will be
directed especially to them, the people in his home town. They
respond angrily when they hear from Jesus what we, Luke's
audience, already know – namely, that as *Son of God* his mission
is universal in its orientation. They are unprepared for this
elucidation of the divine project.

In this developing portrait of Jesus' sonship, the genealogical
affirmation of Jesus' status leads into Jesus' wilderness testing
(4:1–13). Importantly, the focus of those tests has to do with
the nature of his mission as "Son of God." Note how the devil
begins his first and last inquiries, "If you are the Son of God,
then . . ." (4:3, 9). Through this series of temptations, Jesus'
resolve as Son of God is tested. Guided and empowered by the
Spirit (4:1, 14), Jesus faces these tests, proves his fidelity to
God, and so demonstrates his competence to engage in ministry
publicly as God's Son.

Jesus at prayer

A second way in which Jesus' special relationship with God is
highlighted centers on the Lukan portrait of Jesus at prayer. In
fact, as Stephen Barton observes, "the portrayal of Jesus as a
person of prayer, habitually in deep communion with the
Father, especially at points of moment or decision or testing in
his life, and giving his disciples an example to follow, is an
indelible part of Luke's gospel narrative."[14] Significant aspects
of Luke's interest in prayer center on its role in the life of the
disciple and mission of the church;[15] here we are more concerned with how prayer figures in the presentation of Jesus.

[14] Stephen C. Barton, *The Spirituality of the Gospels* (London: SPCK, 1992) 90. On the
theme of prayer in Luke, see Peter T. O'Brien, "Prayer in Luke–Acts," *TynB* 24
(1973) 111–27; Stephen S. Smalley, "Spirit, Kingdom and Prayer in Luke–Acts,"
NovT 15 (1973) 59–71; Allison A. Trites, "The Prayer Motif in Luke–Acts," in
Perspectives on Luke–Acts, 168–86; Steven F. Plymale, *The Prayer Texts of Luke–Acts*,
AUS 7: TR 118 (New York: Peter Lang, 1991); David Crump, *Jesus the Intercessor:
Prayer and Christology in Luke–Acts*, WUNT 2:49 (J. C. B. Mohr [Paul Siebeck],
1992).

[15] On which see below, ch. 5.

Luke employs scenes of Jesus at prayer, first, in order to show how it was in prayer that Jesus experienced and solidified his relationship with God. In a number of the recorded prayers of Jesus, he refers to God specifically as "Father" or "my Father" (10:21–22; 22:41–45; 23:34, 46; cf. 11:2; 22:29), echoing his earlier declaration in the temple at the age of twelve: "Did you not know that I must be in my Father's house?" (2:49). It is in prayer that Jesus hears and embraces the will of God. This is seen most profoundly in the Lukan scene on the Mount of Olives as Jesus anticipates his execution (22:39–46). Here he is about the business of discerning God's purpose, while at the same time determining to submit to God's will. The same motif is probably at work in 6:12–20. Jesus "spent the night in prayer to God," this just prior to his choosing twelve of his followers to be apostles. In choosing the apostles, we are led to believe, Jesus acts on behalf of God, puts God's purpose, discerned in prayer, into action.[16] One may also refer to 3:21, where Jesus receives his divine commission while in prayer.

In prayer, Jesus is strengthened for divine service. Just as he is commissioned, so he receives the guiding and empowering Holy Spirit while in prayer at his baptism (3:21). The scene on the Mount of Olives may also be read in this way, for it was during his struggle in prayer that "an angel from heaven" came to him and strengthened him (22:43). Less obvious but of equal significance is the summary statement of 5:16, which may be translated so as to emphasize that Jesus' act of withdrawing to pray was for him a regular habit: "But he would periodically withdraw to deserted places for the purpose of prayer." Set as it is between reports of Jesus' growing reputation and active ministry, Jesus' habit of prayer is drawn into intimate connection with the more public aspects of his ministry. Apparently we are to see that he prays for strength, and for his ministry to others.

Luke's prayer scenes function in a second way in his Gospel. They not only solidify Jesus' relationship with the Father, but also serve as the arena in which Jesus' status (and so, God's

---

[16] Crump, *Jesus the Intercessor*, 145.

purpose alive in Jesus) is revealed to others. This is most evident in the context of Jesus' prayers on the mount of trans-figuration (9:28–29) and from the cross (23:34,[17] 46), and in Jesus' self-affirmation as the one who reveals the Father in 10:21–24. Because Jesus is God's Son, to overhear him in prayer is to encounter something of God's character and purpose. This motif of disclosure may also be present in the account of Peter's confession of Jesus as "the Messiah of God" in 9:18–20. Significantly, it was "when Jesus was praying alone," that he asked his disciples concerning his identity. Luke thus casts the entire event as a prayer experience in which Jesus' identity is disclosed.[18] Similarly, the identity of the resurrected Jesus is revealed to Cleopas and his friend, not on the Emmaus road, nor even in scriptural exposition (though cf. 24:32), but in the blessing before the meal (24:30–31).[19]

Prayer thus plays a significant role within the Lukan narra-tive. In scenes of prayer, Luke demonstrates in concrete ways for his readers Jesus' experience of and relationship to God as God's Son. Moreover, Luke shows that something of the nature of God's aim and of Jesus' special relationship to God becomes evident to others in the context of Jesus' experience of prayer.

THE IDENTITY OF JESUS IN THE GALILEAN MINISTRY

With Luke 4:14, a new phase of the Third Gospel is begun. Luke 1:5–4:13 introduced Luke's readers to an array of images by which to understand Jesus and the coming to fruition of God's purpose. But these images were mostly suggestive, antici-patory; they looked forward to something else, especially to the public ministry of Jesus. That public ministry begins now, in

---

[17] That 23:34 is original to the Gospel of Luke, in spite of some textual witnesses to the contrary, see Joel B. Green, *The Death of Jesus: Tradition and Interpretation in the Passion Narrative*, WUNT 2:33 (Tübingen: J. C. B. Mohr [Paul Siebeck], 1988) 91–92.

[18] Cf. Luke Timothy Johnson, *The Gospel of Luke*, SP3 (Collegeville, Minnesota: Liturgical, 1991) 150–56.

[19] That 24:30 describes the normal activity of the host or head of the household in the grace before meals, see Joachim Jeremias, *The Eucharistic Words of Jesus* (Philadel-phia: Fortress, 1966) 174–75.

Galilee. It is here that the programmatic beginnings of Jesus' ministry are marked (23:5; Acts 10:37; cf. 13:31). Those earlier chapters outlined what we might expect of God's gracious visitation. With 4:14, we begin to discern not only the *what* but also the *how* of God's purpose. The Galilean segment of Jesus' ministry will extend through 9:50, after which Jesus turns to Jerusalem and begins the long, "travel" section of the Third Gospel. Before the journey to Jerusalem begins, we see in the Galilean segment of Jesus' ministry how Jesus, empowered by the Spirit, understood the nature of his vocation and engaged in its performance by means of a prophetic, itinerant ministry.

Beginning already in his first recorded sermon, at Nazareth, the question of Jesus' identity is posed: "Isn't this the son of Joseph?" (4:22). This is ironic, as we have seen (cf. 1:32–35; 2:48–49; 3:23), but it serves to anticipate the fascination with Jesus' identity throughout this larger section of the Third Gospel. "What kind of utterance is this?" (4:36). "Who is this that speaks such blasphemies" (5:21). "A great prophet has arisen among us!" (7:16). "Are you the one to come . . .?" (7:19–20). "If this man were a prophet . . ." (7:39). "Who is this who even forgives sins?" (7:49). "Who is this, then, that he commands even the winds and the water, and they obey him?" (8:25).

With the onset of ch. 9, the issue of Jesus' identity takes on an enlarged significance as a consequence of *who* broaches the subject. First, we hear from Herod – already known to us for his evil deeds and his imprisonment of John (3:19–20): "John I beheaded; but who is this about whom we hear such things?" (9:9). Interestingly, the answers he has received from the general populace mark Jesus as a prophet (9:7–8). Jesus was anointed as a prophet (4:18–19), he spoke of his prophetic fate (4:24; 13:33), and he identified himself with the prophets Elijah and Elisha (4:25–27). In 7:11–16, he heals the son of a widow, as had Elijah, with the result that the crowds hail him as "a great prophet." Following his death and resurrection, Jesus hears from Cleopas that he was thought to be "a prophet mighty in deed and word" (24:19). What is more, Luke's narration of Jesus' ascension (24:50–51; Acts 1:9–11) is reminiscent of Elijah's ascension in 2 Kings 2:9–15.[20] So the popular answers to the question of Jesus' identity entertained by Herod are not without substance.

Second, Jesus asks his disciples about his identity. Having provided the celebrated identification of Jesus as a prophet (9:18–19), they go on to declare its deficiency. Jesus may be an anointed prophet, but he is much more. He is "the Messiah of God" (9:20). This "something more" comes as no surprise to Luke's readers, who have already seen Jesus compared with John. John was said to be "prophet of the Most High" (1:76), but Jesus is even greater than John.

Third and finally, the matter of Jesus' identity is brought up by God himself. Drawing on language reminiscent of the Scriptures and of the Lukan baptismal scene (3:22), the voice from heaven in the transfiguration episode announces, "This is my Son, my Chosen, listen to him!" (9:35). This divine declaration brings together a constellation of images by which to characterize Jesus. He is "my son," Son of God, the king, son of David, anticipated in the Scriptures and in the angelic announcement (1:32, 35; cf. Ps. 2:7). He is Yahweh's Chosen One, the Servant of Yahweh, who in his suffering and exaltation would serve the purpose of God (Isa. 42:1; cf. Luke 2:32; 23:35).[21] And he is the anticipated Prophet like Moses, the leader of God's people (Deut. 18:15–18; cf. Acts 3:22–26).

Having thus established Jesus' identity with reference to God's own point of view, Luke is now ready to begin his narration of the long and winding journey of Jesus to Jerusalem (9:51–19:27). On the way, Jesus will proclaim his message to disciples and to "the people"/"the crowds," some of whom respond positively and join his followers in receiving instructions for discipleship. On the way Jesus also encounters

---

20 Cf. Gerhard Lohfink, *Die Himmelfahrt Jesu: Untersuchungen zu den Himmelfahrts- und Erhöhungstexten bei Lukas*, SANT 26 (Munich: Kösel, 1971); Thomas L. Brodie, "Luke–Acts as an Imitation and Emulation of the Elijah-Elisha Narrative," in *New Views on Luke and Acts*, ed. Earl Richard (Collegeville, Minnesota: Liturgical, 1990) 78–85, 172–74.

21 See Joel B. Green, "The Death of Jesus, God's Servant," in *Reimaging the Death of the Lukan Jesus*, ed. Dennis D. Sylva, AMTBBB 73 (Frankfurt-on-Main: Anton Hain, 1990) 1–28, 170–73.

increasing opposition that will lead finally to his suffering and death. This, too, must be integrated into our understanding of Jesus in Luke.

First, though, we may focus again on the Galilean ministry of Jesus and its portrayal of Jesus as the anointed leader of God's people. According to his inaugural address in 4:18–19, his mission is to blend together healing, proclamation, and a ministry of "release." In the adjacent account of Jesus' ministry in Capernaum (4:31–43), we begin immediately to see how the contours of this mission will take shape. With authority he both teaches (4:31–32) and commands unclean spirits (4:36), thus putting into effect his prophetic anointing and his activity of "releasing captives" (those who are enslaved to Satan). That is, Jesus does immediately in Capernaum what he pledged in Nazareth.

Subsequent accounts and summary statements of Jesus' ministry repeat and develop this picture of ministry. Summary statements are of particular interest in this regard, since they encapsulate what Luke regards as "typical" of Jesus' ministry. Summaries appear, for example, in 4:37, 44; 5:15–16; 6:18–19; 7:17; 8:1, and highlight three ingredients: Jesus' proclamation, his ministry of healing and exorcism, and his growing reputation among the people.

What does Jesus preach? The fulfillment of God's purpose. Twice Luke summarizes: "the good news of the kingdom of God" (4:43; 8:1). This is a synopsis of Jesus' announcement and activity of God's undertaking: salvation-as-reversal. The message itself is reminiscent of Mary's Song: "he has brought down the powerful . . . and lifted up the lowly" (1:52). Sinners are excluded from the company of the faithful by their sin, but in Jesus' ministry they are forgiven (5:17–26) and invited into a community of discipleship (5:1–11, 27–32). Lepers are excluded from association with other people because of their disease and unclean status before God (Leviticus 14–15), but in Jesus' ministry they are cleansed (5:12–16). A "deserving" Gentile centurion declares his unworthiness, and so has his valued servant healed (7:1–10). A widow, left without any family to protect her with material goods and community status, has her son restored to life (7:11–17). Jesus declares, "Blessed are you who are poor ... but woe to you who are rich" (6:20, 24). And so on. Luke's point is that the ministry of Jesus as prophet-leader, as God's own agent, marks the arrival of God's own benefaction. In Jesus' ministry, God has drawn near with his grace (7:16). Good news, indeed! (cf. Isa. 40:9; 52:7).

As prefigured in the words of Simeon, however, not all will receive the divine prophet with open arms. Jesus himself recognizes the fate of the prophet: rejection (4:24), exclusion and defamation (6:22–23), death (11:47–51; 13:33–34; cf. Neh. 9:26; Acts 7:52).[22] How can the suffering and death of Jesus be integrated with his status as God's own Son, the Servant, the Prophet like Moses?

THE CRUCIFIXION AND EXALTATION OF JESUS

One of the peculiar features of Luke's presentation of Jesus moves beyond Luke's concern to assert the necessity of Jesus' death in order to proclaim that it was precisely as the Messiah that Jesus suffered. It is true that this idea is not absent from the Gospel of Mark,[23] but in Luke's Gospel and Acts we find it stated pointedly and abruptly (24:26; Acts 3:18; 17:3; 26:23). The starkness of this declaration is set in relief by two related observations. First, unlike the other Synoptic Evangelists, Luke seems to have comparably little to say about the motivation behind the cross's centrality; that is, he does not develop its substitutionary importance.[24] Second, the notion of a "suffering messiah" is absent in the Old Testament and in Jewish literature prior to and contemporaneous with Luke–Acts.[25]

---

22 Cf. David E. Aune, *Prophecy in Early Christianity and the Ancient Mediterranean World* (Grand Rapids, Michigan: Wm. B. Eerdmans, 1983) 157–9.

23 See Mark 15 and the discussion in Martin Hengel, *The Atonement: The Origins of the Doctrine in the New Testament* (Philadelphia: Fortress, 1981) 39–47.

24 Thus, Luke neglects to include the "ransom saying" (Mark 10:45; Matt. 20:28) in his Gospel. On this matter, see further Joel B. Green, "'The Message of Salvation' in Luke–Acts," *Ex Auditu* 5 (1989) 21–34 (23–26). On what follows, see Green, "Death of Jesus," in *DJG*, 146–63 (159–61).

25 There is no literary evidence that, prior to Jesus, the equation was made between "Servant (of Yahweh)" and "Messiah"– *contra*, e.g., R. T. France, "Servant of

This has led some scholars to argue that Luke understands the death of Christ as that of a martyr.[26] Though the Lukan passion narrative retains certain themes in common with Jewish tales of martyrdom (e.g., supernatural conflict, divine assistance, the leitmotif of the innocence of the executed, *et al.*), however, others are conspicuous by their absence (e.g., the strong influence of retributive ideas, the repulsive descriptions of torture and death, and the courageous ways in which those facing death embrace their fate). If Luke is not particularly concerned to present Jesus' death as having atoning significance or as a martyrdom, how does he portray the suffering of Christ? How does the suffering and death of Jesus fit into the overall portrayal of Jesus in God's purpose, according to Luke?

The death of Jesus and conflict

The theme of conflict surrounding Jesus' ministry is deeply rooted in the opening chapters of the Gospel. Even while praising God for sending his agent of salvation, Simeon remarks, concerning Jesus, that he will be the cause of a division with Israel: some will respond positively, others negatively to his mission. John promises of the Messiah that he will baptize "with fire" (3:16) – a metaphor that conjures up images of judgment (cf. 3:17; 9:54; 12:49–53; 17:29).

As anticipated, Jesus' ministry attracts opposition, especially as a result of his championing a vision of salvation at odds with that of the religious and political leaders of his world. He is "a friend of tax collectors and sinners" (7:34) and among his disciples he criticizes the *modus operandi* of the Gentile elite, who "lord it over" those of lower status than themselves (22:25). What must not be missed in our reading of such scenes and summary statements in the Third Gospel is the degree to which

Yahweh," in *DJG* 744–7 (745); Joachim Jeremias, "παῖς θεοῦ in Later Judaism in the Period after the LXX," in *TDNT* 5:677–700 (682–700).

[26] See the discussion in Brian E. Beck, "'*Imitatio Christi*' and the Lucan Passion Narrative," in *Suffering and Martyrdom in the New Testament: Studies Presented to G. M. Styler by the Cambridge New Testament Seminar*, ed. William Horbury and Brian McNeil (Cambridge University Press, 1981) 28–47.

Jesus' teaching is thus presented as undercutting the authority and social positions of those who dominate his world. Jesus is doing nothing less than *redefining* the way the world "works." What is more, by grounding his attitudes and behavior in his message of the in-breaking kingdom of God he asserts the divine legitimation of this alternative view of the world.

Luke 4:16–30 records in a paradigmatic way the response Jesus' message will provoke: his own townspeople are scandalized by his message and threaten to kill him. Elsewhere in the Gospel, it is especially the Jewish leadership who are aligned against Jesus, and among them, especially the chief priests. Herod, too, is cast in this role (13:32). Even Pilate, who seems convinced of Jesus' innocence (23:4, 14, 22), joins the opposition against Jesus and hands him over to be crucified (23:25).

Lurking behind the scenes throughout this tale of conflict is the chief opposition against God's purpose, and so against Jesus who unswervingly serves that purpose. This is Satan, who becomes in the Lukan passion narrative a key player. He has been present throughout the ministry of Jesus (cf., e.g., 13:10–17), but now, by entering into Judas (22:3), he gains a beachhead from which to attack Jesus from within the inner circle of Jesus' followers. From there he threatens the integrity of the circle of disciples (22:31), tests Jesus in his resolve to proceed in obedience to God (22:39–46),[27] and is even implicated in the arrest of Jesus (22:53).[28]

In these ways, Luke outlines the fundamental point that the gracious visitation of God does not occur without resistance from diabolic forces. These forces manifest themselves in the opposition of human parties to the mission and message of Jesus. And the consequence of this eschatological, cosmic hostility is the death of Jesus. If this is true of God's Son, will it not also be true of his disciples? Indeed, with the passion approaching, Jesus declares that a new time has come when his followers engaged in itinerant ministry will not be able to depend on normal Mediterranean hospitality; they too will encounter

---

[27] In 22:28, 40, 46 the term πειρασμός is employed to designate the diabolic character of the "testing" described; cf. 4:13; 8:13.

[28] "Power of darkness" signifies the realm of Satan – cf. the parallelism in Acts 26:18: "to turn from darkness to light and from the power of Satan to God."

hostility (22:35–38; cf. 12:51–53).[29] Importantly, Jesus links this conflict directly to scriptural fulfillment:

For I tell you, this scripture must be fulfilled in me: "And he was counted among the lawless." Indeed what is written about me is being fulfilled. (22:38)

The death of Jesus and Jesus' sonship

If Luke goes to such great lengths to endorse the *necessity* of Jesus' passion, this is only because he understands the suffering of Jesus as integral to Jesus' identity as Son of God. We have already noted the degree to which the beginnings of Jesus' ministry are permeated with his characterization as Son of God. We may add to this a further realization – namely, as Jesus nears his execution his status as Son of God is again highlighted.

After entering Jerusalem, while teaching in the area of the temple, he tells a parable that anticipates the slaying of the "beloved son" (20:9–19), an unmistakable intertextual reference to God's characterization of Jesus at his baptism: "You are my Son, the Beloved" (3:22). He goes on to act as his Father's representative, conferring on his disciples a kingdom (22:29). As Jesus struggles in prayer on the Mount of Olives, he addresses God as "Father"; moreover, as a true son, he does so in order obediently to represent the will of the Father in the course of his own life (22:42–44). His prayers from the cross are addressed to God as Father, and build on the christological picture painted earlier in the Gospel. Now Jesus is portrayed as one who discloses the Father's mercy (cf. 6:32–36) and who trusts in his Father's faithfulness (23:34, 46).

The death of Jesus and discipleship

Jesus' final act of entrusting himself fully to his Father did not go unrewarded. Luke 24 narrates the discovery of Jesus' empty

---

[29] See G. W. H. Lampe, "The Two Swords (Luke 22:35–8)," in *Jesus and the Politics of His Day*, ed. Ernst Bammel and C. F. D. Moule (Cambridge University Press, 1984) 335–51.

tomb, his post-resurrection appearances, and, finally, Jesus'
ascension. Luke will interpret Jesus' resurrection and ascension
as his being "raised up," his exaltation. Among the many
transpositions that so characterize his Gospel, herein we come
face-to-face with what is for Luke the definitive reversal: the
Righteous One (23:47),[30] repeatedly declared innocent by the
Roman authorities (23:4, 14–15, 22), is executed in the way
reserved for those of low status, by crucifixion, only to be raised
up by God. God raises up the lowly, vindicates the faithful.

On the one hand, then, Jesus' death emphasizes the hostility
to be encountered by those who proclaim God's coming as a
reversal of status. Those who are self-seeking, those who are
concerned with ensuring their own high status in society – such
people do not receive Jesus' message gladly. The ensuing
conflict leads to the cross. On the other hand, in a profoundly
ironic way, the passion of Jesus is joined by his exaltation, and
these together embody in an ultimate way the salvation-as-
reversal theme that threads its way throughout the Gospel of
Luke.[31] The passion of Jesus is thus a call to vigilance and
fidelity as well as a promise of salvation.

JESUS, LUKE, AND THE JEWISH PEOPLE

If Luke's presentation of God's purpose arises out of the
ancient promises to Israel, what is the place of Israel now in the
fulfillment of God's promises? If Jesus is God's own representative, why is he opposed by many of the leaders of God's own
people? Here arises one of the more pressing issues of Lukan
theology,[32] for the Gospel of Luke does not appear to speak
with only one voice on this issue. One might be tempted to
attribute the consequent tension within the Third Gospel to a

---

30 Some translations render the centurion's words, ὁ ἄνθρωπος οὗτος δίκαιος ἦν, as
    "this man was innocent"; see, however, the collocation of "Righteous One" and
    language descriptive of Jesus' suffering and death, drawing on Isa. 52:13–53:12, in
    Acts 3:13–18.
31 Green, "The Death of Jesus, God's Servant"; cf. Richard Glöckner, *Die Verkündi-
    gung des Heils beim Evangelisten Lukas*, WS 9 (Mainz: Matthias-Grünewald, 1976).
32 For a helpful entry into this discussion, see Joseph B. Tyson, ed., *Luke–Acts and the
    Jewish People: Eight Critical Perspectives* (Minneapolis: Augsburg, 1988).

disparity between Luke's sources and his own creative contribution; first, however, it is worth asking whether Luke's perspective on the Jewish people might be rooted precisely at the intersection of these two apparently disparate viewpoints.

First impressions

One of the primary obstacles to deciphering Luke's stance *vis-à-vis* Judaism is the wide array of relevant data. One cannot afford to focus only, for example, on those texts that speak of "the Jews" (there are only five occurrences of "Jews" or "Jewish" – 7:3; 23:3, 37, 38, 51). There are Jewish institutions (e.g., the temple and synagogue), Jewish practices (e.g., fasting and Sabbath-keeping), Jewish Scriptures (e.g., "the law and the prophets" as well as "law" used in the more technical, normative sense), Jewish hopes for deliverance or dominion, and there are varieties of character groups within the Jewish people (e.g., scribes, Pharisees, priests). To complicate things further, it is possible at least in theory that, within Luke's world, each character group may have within it variations (i.e., some Pharisees may respond differently than others), and each may have its own ways of articulating faithfulness with respect to Jewish institutions, practices, Scriptures, and so on. Even within the world of Luke's Gospel, then, one must not move too quickly to speak of "the Jews" as a monolithic group.[33]

This is not to say, however, that one cannot speak of general impressions. (1) Luke portrays Israel as God's people – those to whom he had made covenant promises and through whom the promised salvation would come (e.g., 1:54–55, 72). (2) Luke portrays Israel as a people in need, a people struggling with the shape of their faith in the context of Roman occupation. They long for deliverance, for God's gracious intervention (e.g.,

---

[33] This is a major failing, e.g., of Jack Dean Kingsbury, *Conflict in Luke: Jesus, Authorities, Disciples* (Philadelphia: Fortress, 1991), and John H. Elliott, "Temple Versus Household in Luke–Acts: A Contrast in Social Institutions," in Jerome H. Neyrey, ed., *The Social World of Luke–Acts: Models for Interpretation* (Peabody, Massachusetts, Hendrickson, 1991) 211–40.

1:68–75; 2:25, 38; 7:16). (3) Luke portrays Israel as a people in need of repentance – that is, of a fresh orientation of life around the purpose of God. Gabriel predicts of John that "he will turn many of the people of Israel to the Lord their God" (1:16). This need is repeated in the Song of Zechariah (1:76–79), and is implicit in John's message of repentance and invitation to Jews to participate in a repentance-baptism (3:3–14). (4) Finally, early on Luke portrays Israel prospectively as a divided people, divided in their future responses to the visitation of God in Jesus' ministry (2:34–35). This division is then played out in the Lukan narrative in the person of the crowds that follow and surround Jesus. These crowds are made up of potential believers (e.g., 9:10–11), but they may misunderstand his ministry (12:54–56) and may even be associated with his execution (22:47; 23:4, 18, 35).

Negative and positive images

Beyond such general impressions one finds both negative and positive images. The scribes/lawyers/teachers of the law, for example, are consistently portrayed in a role antagonistic toward Jesus. They question and test Jesus (5:17, 21; 10:25; 11:53), complain about him (5:30; 15:2), look for a way to accuse and execute him (6:7; 19:47; 20:19; 22:2), and participate in his execution (9:22; 22:66; 23:10). Even the apparently positive assessment of Jesus by "some of the scribes" in 20:39, while potentially opening the door of rehabilitation for individual scribes, is quickly tempered by the question posed by Jesus to the scribes in 20:41–44 and especially by his scathing criticism in 20:46: "Beware of the scribes . . .!" (cf. 11:46, 52). Interestingly, they seem also to influence others in the narrative negatively; although Luke's portrait of the Pharisees on their own terms is capable of interesting subtlety, when they appear in tandem with these experts on the law Pharisees are always presented as Jesus' adversaries (see 5:17, 21, 30; 6:7; 7:30; 11:53; 14:3; 15:2).

A second example of the negative disposition Luke can assume with respect to Judaism is represented by scenes in which the Jewish synagogue figures prominently. Although Jesus habitually goes to the synagogue on the Sabbath (4:16; cf. 4:31–33; 6:6; 13:10) and teaches there (4:16–30, 44), the Third Gospel grows in its pessimism concerning the possibility of the synagogue's standing as an instrument of God's will. Jesus encounters opposition from the synagogue in Nazareth (4:16–30); his healing on the Sabbath in the synagogue in 6:6–11 is met with hostility; and in 13:10–17 the synagogue and its leadership seem actually to conspire to exclude the possibility of healing for the woman bent over. In 12:11 and 21:12 the synagogue is named as the site of eschatological persecution of the disciples; and in 11:43; 20:46 the synagogue is the setting for the disclosure of the hypocrisy of the Pharisees and scribes. Although Paul and others will enter the synagogue as a missionary strategy in Acts, the same pattern is developed: rejection in the synagogue, and, in some cases, the subsequent success of a parallel ministry in the home (e.g., Acts 18:4–8, 26).

A final example is Luke's presentation of the Jewish leaders in Jerusalem, and especially of the Jerusalem-based priesthood. An immediate exception to this overall negative portrayal is the introduction of Zechariah in Luke 1:5–20. He, together with his wife, was blameless, righteous. But this is less an exception than one might think – first, because even this righteous priest proves slow to believe the good news from God delivered by Gabriel (contrast the submission of Mary, a peasant girl, to God's purpose [1:38]); and second because Zechariah is not one of the priestly elites centered in Jerusalem, but rather a village priest in the Judean hills (1:39). Otherwise, priests appear negatively – juxtaposed along with the Roman authorities over against John, God's prophet (3:1–6); unwilling to assist someone in need (10:31); and actively present in the suffering and death of Jesus (9:22, 47; 20:1, 19; 22:2, 4, 50, 52, 54, 66; 23:4, 10, 13; 24:20).

Alongside these one must also place the impressively positive images of Judaism represented in the world of Luke. Luke 1–2 is teeming with such images: the importance of faithful obedience to the law (1:5–7; 2:22–39); portraits of Jewish piety such as prayer, worship, fasting, and expectant waiting (1:10, 13,

25, 46–55, 69–79; 2:13, 14, 20, 25, 37, 38); the representation of life oriented around the Jerusalem temple (e.g., 1:8–10, 21–23; 2:22–51).

More broadly we may mention the dependence of Luke on the Scriptures of Israel and the emphasis within the narrative on Moses and the prophets. Earlier,[34] we drew attention to Luke's strategy of drawing the Scriptures into his story of Jesus so as to assert the ministry of Jesus as the continuation of the story of God and God's people in the Old Testament. In fact, there are important texts wherein it appears that Luke believes that the Scriptures, if only understood correctly, are all that is needed for faithful living. The extravagantly wealthy man who begs Abraham to send Lazarus back to warn his brothers of their impending peril is told, "If they do not listen to Moses and the prophets, neither will they be convinced even if someone rises from the dead" (16:31). What is of particular import about this statement is that, in Luke's discourse situation – that is, at the time and under the circumstances of his writing – someone has risen from the dead. Will people continue to misread Moses and the prophets, and so fail to perceive God's purpose and the significance of the events of Jesus' life, death, and exaltation? Similarly, Jesus claims that what he has accomplished is nothing more than what was written about him in Moses, the prophets, and the psalms (24:44). The Scriptures are not set aside (cf. 16:17), even if they must be understood correctly, interpreted appropriately. Here is a clue to help us grasp the place of Judaism in Luke's theology.

The Pharisees in Luke's Gospel

By way of struggling with the variegated presentation of Judaism in Luke's world, we may focus finally on his presentation of the Pharisees. Taken on their own terms, the Pharisees (in whom Luke is manifestly interested) provide a window into the wider portrayal of Judaism in the Gospel of Luke.

In the Third Gospel, the Pharisees are known above all for

[34] See above, ch. 2

two character traits. First, they are repeatedly depicted as an interpretive community, concerned with the faithful embodiment of the law in daily behavior. They are concerned with propriety, and for this reason are often at odds with Jesus: his interpretation, and thus his practices, are unconventional when compared with theirs. He associates with toll-collectors and sinners (5:30; 7:39; 15:2), fails to keep the Sabbath (6:2, 7; 14:3), does not wash his hands before eating (11:38), and his disciples fail to fast (5:33). In all of these ways and more, Jesus, from the point of view of the Pharisees in Luke, demonstrates his lack of regard for scriptural holiness. For his part, Jesus regards the Pharisees as insufficiently scriptural: "But woe to you Pharisees! You tithe mint and rue and herbs of all sorts, and neglect the justice and love of God" (11:42; cf. 11:39).

Second, Pharisees are presented as persons concerned with self-promotion. According to Jesus' indictment, they love seats of honor in the synagogue and to receive first greetings in the marketplace (11:43). Jesus even tells the story of a Pharisee who in prayer distinguishes himself from "thieves, rogues, adulterers" and toll-collectors and so asserts his own status as a righteous man (18:9–14). As narrator, Luke describes Pharisees as "lovers of money," calling attention to the desire of Pharisees to achieve high status by serving as wealthy benefactors to those in need (16:14).[35]

On the other hand, it is consequential that Jesus joins Pharisees in table fellowship (7:36; 11:37; 14:1) – and that in a Gospel where table fellowship is so positive in its implications of proffered grace and redemptive association. Even the seemingly irreversible criticism of the Pharisees – that they "rejected God's purpose for themselves" (7:30) – is tempered by the subsequent presence of Jesus at the table of a Pharisee. This suggests a fundamental openness on the part of Jesus in Luke to the ongoing possibility that Pharisees will join him in fellowship and service.[36] In fact, in 13:31 "some Pharisees" do

[35] On this interpretation, see Halvor Moxnes, *The Economy of the Kingdom: Social Conflict and Economic Relations in Luke's Gospel*, OBT (Philadelphia: Fortress, 1988).

[36] John A. Darr (*On Character Building: The Reader and the Rhetoric of Characterization in Luke–Acts*, LCBI [Louisville, Kentucky: Westminster/John Knox, 1992] esp. chs.

side with Jesus over against Herod.[37] And the Pharisees are not in any way implicated by Luke's narrative in the suffering and death of Jesus.

In Luke's portrayal of the Pharisees, the primary issue is hypocrisy; thus Jesus warns his disciples, "Beware of the yeast of the Pharisees – that is, their hypocrisy" (12:1). In contemporary parlance, this might be taken to suggest that the Pharisees in Luke's Gospel are insincere or dishonest, but this view is almost certainly not supported by Luke's narrative. "Hypocrisy" is a transliteration of the Greek term ὑπόκρισις, used in the LXX for "a person whose conduct is not determined by God and is thus 'godless.'"[38] The point, then, is that in Luke Jesus regards the Pharisees as misdirected in their pursuit of scriptural faithfulness. At present they are working at cross-purposes with Jesus, but this does not render them as irredeemable. For now, though, they lack what is necessary to interpret the Scriptures correctly. They do not understand God's purpose and so, however sincere and honest in their struggle to obey God, they can only give the impression of piety. It is in this sense that they are hypocrites.

This is a further reminder of our discussion in chapter 2 of the relation of God's purpose to the Scriptures. We may recall that fundamental for Luke is God's purpose, with the Scriptures giving expression to that purpose. Now we see that in the hands of such characters in Luke as the Pharisees, the Scriptures do not necessarily yield the redemptive story of God. The Scriptures can be read erroneously. Concerned with their own agenda and status-seeking, the Pharisees mold the Scriptures to

1–2, 4) argues that Luke "builds" characters progressively, so that the possibility alluded to here would be ruled out by the previously negative portrayal of the Pharisees. Johnson (*Luke*, 217–18) seems to argue similarly. What, then, is one to make of Paul, a Pharisee in Acts who embraces and serves God's purpose? In fact, characterization is not only progressive; one must leave room for retrospective modification.

[37] Cf. parallel expressions of care in Acts 21:12–14, whose presence in the Lukan narrative speaks against Johnson's reading of the present warning as a hostile test (*Luke*, 221).

[38] Heinz Giesen, "ὑπόκρισις, ὑποκρίνομαι," in *EDNT*, 3:403; cf. Robert H. Smith, "Hypocrite," in *DJG*, 351–53; Job 34:30; 36:13; 2 Macc. 6:21–25; 4 Macc. 6:15–23; *Pss. Sol.* 4:5–6, 22.

an alternative purpose, one that fails to account for God's justice and love (11:42; cf. ch. 14). In the hands of the Pharisees, then, we see the Scriptures and, along with them, other things Jewish (including the Pharisees themselves!), in their full ambiguity for Luke. The religion of Israel – its institutions, practices, and so on – is to be embraced fully when understood *vis-à-vis* the redemptive purpose of God. But in order to be understood thus, Israel's religion must cohere with the purpose of God as articulated by God's own authorized interpretive and redemptive agent, God's Son, Jesus of Nazareth.

CHAPTER 4

"To proclaim good news to the poor":
mission and salvation

ANNOUNCEMENT IN NAZARETH

It has become axiomatic in studies of Luke that Jesus' sermon at Nazareth (4:16–30) is programmatic for our understanding of the mission of Jesus in the Gospel.[1] Its importance is suggested by a number of factors. First, unlike the other Synoptic Evangelists (Matt. 13:53–58; Mark 6:1–6), Luke has located Jesus' ministry in Nazareth not in the midst of the Galilean ministry but at its beginning. Indeed, following lengthy anticipations and preparations (1:5–4:13), this is the first scene of Jesus' public ministry. Here are his first spoken words in the Gospel. Second, although it was customary for Jesus to attend the synagogue and teach on the Sabbath (4:15, 16, 31–37, 44; 6:6; 13:10–17), nowhere else do we hear of the content of his teaching. Consequently, his message here serves as an exemplar of his synagogue teaching more generally. Third, summaries of Jesus' ministry in Luke–Acts refer back to this episode as paradigmatic for our understanding of Jesus' vocation (7:18–23; Acts 10:38). Finally, the *content* of Jesus' message at Nazareth is as momentous as is its setting at the onset of his

---

[1] See the excellent survey of the discussion on Luke 4:16–30 in Christopher J. Schreck, "The Nazareth Pericope: Luke 4:16–30 in Recent Study," in *L'Evangile de Luc – The Gospel of Luke*, revised and enlarged edition of *L'Evangile de Luc: Problémes littéraires et théologiques*, ed. F. Neirynck, BETL 32 (Leuven University Press, 1989) 399–471. On what follows, see Joel B. Green, "'Proclaiming Repentance and Forgiveness of Sins to all Nations': A Biblical Perspective on the Church's Mission," in *The World is My Parish: The Mission of the Church in Methodist Perspective*, ed. Alan G. Padgett, SHM 10 (Lewiston, New York: Edwin Mellen, 1992) 24–33.

public ministry. In these words the shape of Jesus' ministry in the Third Gospel is given form.[2] What is this message?

Some interpreters have hoped to find the key to understanding this pericope by taking with utmost seriousness its intertextual relationship to the Isaianic material.[3] This is surely true along general lines, but one must also account for the fact that the Isaianic citation is, in Luke 4:18–19, already *re-interpreted*. This is true both because of its new narrative setting within the Lukan narrative but also because it is not a word-for-word citation. In fact, in borrowing from the septuagintal version of Isaiah 61:1–2, Luke has omitted an important phrase, "the day of vengeance of our God" (Isa. 61:2b), and added from Isa. 58:6 a further descriptive phrase, "to send forth the oppressed in release."[4] The result is the suppression of a potential focus on the theme of judgment or retribution, and the following structure:

> The Spirit of the Lord is upon <u>me</u>,
>   for he has anointed <u>me</u>;
> To preach good news to the poor he has sent <u>me</u>:
>   To proclaim for the captives *release*,
>   and to the blind sight;
>   To send forth the oppressed in *release*;
>   To proclaim the year of the Lord's favor.

This more literal translation draws particular attention to the emphatic position of the repeated terms "me" and "release," and thus to the importance of the theme of "release" in Jesus' message.

The emphasis on "me" must be read against the background of the build-up of anticipation regarding Jesus' identity and public ministry. The narrative has narrowed the spotlight on

---

[2] One might add that, insofar as 4:16–30 anticipates a mission to the Gentiles, it establishes narrative needs not resolved in the Third Gospel; hence, in an important sense, 4:16–30 looks ahead not only to Jesus' ministry but also to that of the church in Acts.

[3] See, e.g., David Peter Seccombe, *Possessions and the Poor in Luke–Acts*, SNTU B6 (Linz: Fuchs, 1983) ch. 2.

[4] On these and other innovations in the citation of the Isaianic text, see Darrell L. Bock, *Proclamation from Prophecy and Pattern: Lucan Old Testament Christology*, JSNTSS 12 (Sheffield: JSOT, 1987) 105–11.

Jesus as the anointed one, the regal, prophetic figure who will work under the guidance of, and as empowered by, the Spirit of the Lord.

The ministry of "release"

The emphasis on "release," together with the final appeal to "the year of the Lord's favor," inscribes the present text not only in Isa. 58:6; 61:1–2, but, more deeply, in legislation related to the Jubilee in Leviticus 25. According to Lev. 25:10, the year of Jubilee is "the year of release." Jubilee was a reminder that God was sovereign over the land and that the reign of God entailed freedom from bondage. Accordingly, every fiftieth year property would be returned to the original owners, debts would be canceled, and those Jews who had managed their debts by selling themselves into slavery would be released. Although there is no material evidence of the actual, historical execution of the Jubilee legislation, this does not mean it was forgotten by Israel. Isaiah 58:6; 61:1–2 and the Melchizedek scroll from Qumran (11QMelch) both attest an eschatological re-interpretation of Leviticus 25, likening the epoch of salvation to the eschatological Jubilee. Luke, then, has represented Jesus' opening address at Nazareth as an announcement of the final Jubilee, the new era of salvation, the breaking-in of God's kingdom.

As it is developed subsequently in the Lukan narrative, "release" comes to have focused meaning. On the one hand, "release" entails "forgiveness" (literally, "release from sins").[5] Luke presents Jesus as the Savior who grants forgiveness of sins. On the other, the power of "release" at work in Jesus' ministry nullifies the binding power of Satan (cf. Acts 8:22–23; 10:38). Almost every account of healing in the Third Gospel is portrayed as an encounter with diabolic forces,[6] but this is particularly evident in 13:10–17: "Ought not this woman, this

---

[5] See the use of ἄφεσις/ἀφίημι ("release, forgiveness" / "to release, to forgive") in 1:77; 3:3; 5:20–21, 23–24; 7:47–49; 11:4; 12:10; 17:3–4; 23:34; 24:47.

[6] See Ulrich Busse, *Die Wunder des Propheten Jesu: Rezeption, Komposition und Interpretation der Wundertradition im Evangelium des Lukas*, FB 24 (Stuttgart: Katholisches Bibelwerk, 1977).

daughter of Abraham, whom Satan has bound for eighteen long years, be set free from this bondage on the Sabbath?"

Lest we fail to appreciate the far-reaching importance of the release effected in Jesus' ministry, we should note that Luke portrays both forgiveness and healing in social terms to match their more evident spiritual and physical overtones. What is forgiveness but removing the barrier (sin) that had previously excluded one from one's community? And what is healing, if not at least the removal of the barrier (sickness, uncleanness) that had kept one from one's own community? "Release" for Luke signifies wholeness, freedom from diabolic and social chains, acceptance.

Jesus' words concerning "the blind" in 4:18 reflect a similar concern with literal and larger meaning. Recovery of sight is in the Lukan narrative clearly an issue of physical healing (cf. 18:35–43; Acts 9:18–19), but it is also presented as a metaphor for receiving revelation and experiencing salvation and inclusion in God's family (cf., e.g., 1:78–79; 2:9, 29–32; 3:6; 6:39–42; 8:35–43; 10:23–24; 11:29–36; 19:1–10; 24:31; *et al.*).[7]

Good news to the poor

The way we have punctuated Jesus' citation of the Isaianic material calls attention to a further Lukan emphasis. The three infinitive clauses – "to proclaim ..., to send forth ..., to proclaim ..." – are all interpretations of the first, "to preach good news to the poor he has sent me." In other words, "to preach good news to the poor" is Jesus' own statement of primary mission in the Gospel of Luke, with the other clauses working to flesh out something of how this primary mission takes shape.

Who are the "poor"? What does it mean "to preach good news" to such people? These are important questions for Luke, since they stand here at the head of Jesus' missionary self-understanding. Our tendency today is to define "the poor" economically, on a scale of annual household income or with

---

[7] See Dennis Hamm, "Sight to the Blind: Vision as Metaphor in Luke," *Bib* 67 (1986) 457–77. On blindness as a metaphor for spiritual imperception, see 9:45; 18:34; 19:42; 24:16.

reference to an established, national or international poverty line. But this is only another reflection of our tendency to read our own world back into Luke's.

A helpful way forward has been presented by Howard Eilberg-Schwartz, who has drawn attention to the different ways in which status and purity were measured in priestly, early Christian, and Dead Sea communities.[8] He notes, first, a continuum on which communities might be placed so as to signify how they measure relative status. On the one end is "ascription," a focus on which would lead one to measure status as an actual property of the external world. One has no control over "ascribed status"; it is imputed on the basis of family heritage, one's sex, and other inherited/genetic attributes. Balancing ascription is "performance," whereby status would be granted as a consequence of one's actions – say, by means of education or conformity to prescribed behaviors.

What has this to do with Jesus' mission to "the poor"? Already we have shifted the discussion away from economic class and opened up the possibility that status in a community might be measured in quite different ways in antiquity than is the case in many Western societies. In fact, according to texts like Lev. 21:16–24, within the community of priests status was measured above all by *ascription*, not performance. First, no one chose to be a priest, but was born into a priestly family. Second, numerous genetic "defects" could result in exclusion from priestly status:

Blemish	Blind	Lame	Mutilated Face/Limb
Broken Foot	Hunchback		Blemish in Eyes
Dwarf	Itching Disease	Scabs	Crushed Testicles

Although membership in the Dead Sea community was related to performance, so that all potentially new members underwent probationary testing to determine their worthiness, the community also emphasized ascription. Only those of Israelite descent were allowed entry. Moreover, according to the Rule

---

[8] Howard Eilberg-Schwartz, *The Savage in Judaism: An Anthropology of Israelite Religion and Ancient Judaism* (Bloomington: Indiana University Press, 1990) 195–216. By "early Christian" Eilberg-Schwartz means "Pauline," but his framework is nonetheless suggestive for our reading of Luke.

of the Congregation, persons could be excluded from the congregation of the whole assembly as a result of injury or genetic fault (1QSa 2.5–7) – for example:

Afflicted in the Flesh   Injured Feet or Hands
Lame   Blind   Deaf   Dumb

And the War Scroll excludes such persons as the following from joining in the eschatological battle:

Boys   Women   Lame   Blind   Crippled
Permanent Bodily Defect or Bodily Impurity.[9]

Ascription-based factors such as these, factors over which one had no control, predetermined a person's status as an outsider *vis-à-vis* priestly and Dead Sea communities.

There are similar lists in Luke, but their purpose is far different. Whereas these priestly and Qumranic texts list those who are impure and of low status because of disability so as to exclude them, Luke presents such lists in order to indicate the very people who should be included.[10] In fact, seven of the ten occurrences of the word "poor" (πτωχός) in Luke appear in lists of this nature:

4:18	*6:20*	*7:22*	*14:13*
Poor	Poor	Blind	Poor
Captive	Hungry	Lame	Maimed
Blind	Mournful	Leper	Lame
Oppressed	Persecuted	Deaf	Blind
		Dead	
		Poor	

14:21	*16:20, 22*
Poor	Poor
Maimed	Ulcerated
Blind	Hungry
Lame	

[9] Cf. J. A. Sanders, "The Ethics of Election in Luke's Great Banquet Parable," in *Essays in Old Testament Ethics: J. Phillip Hyatt, In Memoriam*, ed James L. Crenshaw and John T. Willis (New York: Ktav, 1974) 245–71. Eilberg-Schwartz (*Savage in Judaism*, 207–8) notes that at Qumran performance was sometimes in competition with ascription – e.g., CD 13.3.

[10] See Joel B. Green, "Good News to Whom? Jesus and the 'Poor' in the Gospel of Luke," in *Jesus of Nazareth: Lord and Christ. Essays on the Historical Jesus and New*

This accumulation of adjectives in their narrative settings draws special attention (1) to the nature of those who are the unexpected recipients of good news (4:16–30; 7:18–23) and blessedness (6:20–26), and (2) to the status of the normally excluded who are now to be welcomed (14:12–14, 15–24; 16:19–31). In each case "poor" stands at the head of the list, except in 7:22 where it appears in the final, emphatic position. "Poor" thus interprets and is amplified by the others. Apparently, Luke is concerned above all with a category of people ordinarily defined above all by their dishonorable status, their exclusion.

This insight is underscored by the use of the vocabulary of wealth in the Third Gospel. One thinks immediately of 1:51–53, where the proud and mighty are contrasted with the humble, the rich (who are well fed) with the hungry. Similarly, in 12:16–21 and 16:19–31 the rich are those who fail to consider the plight of others in spite of their own extravagant resources. Perhaps most interesting is 14:12: "rich neighbors" are listed with one's "inner circle" – friends, brothers, kin – persons with whom one enjoys relationships of equality and mutuality. Like "poor," then, "rich" is not simply an economic term; it is related to issues of power and privilege, and social location as an insider.

"Preaching good news to the poor," then, entails a focus for Jesus' ministry on overturning previous measures of status. Unlike the priestly and Qumran communities – indeed, unlike the wider Jewish world of Luke's Gospel – people are not to be predetermined as insiders or outsiders by their sex, family heritage, financial position, location in the city or in rural environs, religious purity, and so on. The message of Jesus is that such status markers are no longer binding. Anyone may freely receive the grace of God. Anyone may join the community of Jesus' followers. All are welcome.

This is not a view easily accepted. Jesus' own townspeople

Testament Christology, ed. Joel B. Green and Max Turner (Grand Rapids, Michigan: Wm. B. Eerdmans, 1994) 59–74.

do not understand it at first, and when they do they respond angrily, violently toward Jesus. Their question, "Is not this Joseph's son?", is what we would expect; Luke has already informed us that the public assumed that Jesus was son of Joseph (3:23). But in this identification the people of Nazareth are caught in a case of situational irony, for they respond to Jesus according to their own parochial understanding. Jesus' auditors recognize in his gracious words good news for themselves. They see themselves as the immediate beneficiaries of the Lord's favor, for they claim Jesus as the son of Joseph, "the son of one of our own" – indeed, as "one of us." But in thinking thus they fall casualty to a subtle joke between narrator and reader. *We* (Luke's readers outside the narrative) know that their understanding of Jesus is erroneous, for we know that Jesus is Son of God, not son of Joseph; he comes to fulfill the purpose of God, not to be restricted either by the demands of the devil (4:1–13) or, now, by those of his own townspeople (4:16–30). Jesus himself is aware of these narrow expectations, and unveils them in his response. "You will quote ... you will say" in 4:23 indicates Jesus' inside knowledge of the thoughts of his audience, whereby he draws out the implications of the audience's reaction in the present. "Doctor, cure yourself!" was a well-known maxim in antiquity,[11] one that could be employed in an argument to insist that one must not refuse to do to one's own relations the favors one does to others, or that one must not benefit others while refusing the same benefits to one's own relations. Jesus addresses the parochial vision of his townspeople head on, countering their assumptions that, as Joseph's son, he will be especially for them a source of God's favor. His is a ministry to all, and especially, according to 4:18–19, to those who have no claim to status,

---

[11] See most recently John Nolland, "Classical Rabbinic Parallels to 'Physician, Heal Yourself' (Luke iv 23)," *NovT* 21 (1979) 193–209; and especially the appendix to S. J. Noorda, "'Cure Yourself, Doctor!' (Luke 4,23): Classical Parallels to an Alleged Saying of Jesus," in *Logia: Les Paroles de Jésus–The Sayings of Jesus. Mémorial Joseph Coppens*, ed. Joël Delobel, BETL 59 (Leuven University Press, 1982) 459–67 (466–67).

who have no claim to belonging to the group of those favored
by God.

That Jesus' vocation of "proclaiming good news to the poor"
embraces not only the economically oppressed in particular
but also the excluded and disadvantaged of society more generally becomes clear from a survey of Jesus' interactions with
people in the Third Gospel. Indeed, it is surely of consequence
that, though Jesus announces his mission "to the poor," Luke
never narrates his actually evangelizing "the poor" so
named.[12] Instead, Jesus is continuously in the company of
those on the margins of society, able neither to participate as
full partners in social interchange nor completely rejected.

The mission of Jesus

In addition to 4:16–30, examined above, two other Lukan
accounts highlight the character of Jesus' mission – the calling
of Levi (5:27–32) and the quest of Zacchaeus (19:1–10).[13]
These stories share many common elements: (1) both narrate
the encounter of Jesus with a toll-collector; (2) both disclose
the low status of toll-collectors, even naming them as "sinners"
(5:30; 19:7); (3) both illustrate behavior becoming a disciple –
Levi by leaving everything, following Jesus, and throwing a
feast in Jesus' honor; Zacchaeus by making fourfold restitution

---

[12] It might be argued that Luke's "people/crowds" should be equated with
"peasants," and that "peasants" are "the poor"; but this only begs the question
whether this (i.e., "peasant") or any other social group in the ancient Mediterranean world (at least) can be defined solely with reference to economic terms. That
such an exercise is futile in the case of peasants see Teador Shanin, ed., *Peasants and
Peasant Societies: Selected Readings*, 2nd ed. (London: Basil Blackwell, 1987). One
might refer to 6:20 ("you poor") as a direct address by Jesus to "the poor."
However, 6:24 ("you rich") must also be taken into account, and attempts to argue
for an audience in 6:24 other than one including the disciples have not been
convincing. Nor need "leaving everything" necessarily imply one's acquiring
economic impoverishment, as 5:28–29 makes clear. The material in 6:22–23
regarding exclusion from the people also speaks against a narrow, economic reading
here.

[13] On what follows, see Green, "Good News to Whom?"

to those he has defrauded and giving half of his goods to the poor; and (4) both generalize from this encounter to clarify the contours of Jesus' mission: "I have not come to call the righteous but sinners to repentance" (5:32); and "For the Son of Man came to seek and to save the lost" (19:10).

In these texts, the unenviably low social status of toll-collectors throughout Roman antiquity is presumed – and even furthered – by the additional description of Levi and Zacchaeus as "sinners." As James Dunn has documented, in the factional context of the era in question a "sinner" would be one whose behavior departs from the norms of an identified group whose boundaries are established with reference to characteristic conduct.[14] That is, "sinner" receives concrete explication especially in terms of group definition; a "sinner" is an outsider.

This concern with group boundaries is transparent in both of these accounts. First, Luke reports the shock of the bystanders at Jesus' willingness to eat with Levi and his guests. Regarded as persons of lower status (due, e.g., to their perceived religious impurity and law-breaking practices), they were to be avoided, especially at the table. Moreover, Luke 5:27–32 is narrated in such a way as to indicate that Jesus' opponents have one view of things, the narrator and Jesus another. Jesus' associates at the table are regarded as "toll-collectors and *sinners*" by the Pharisees and teachers of the law, whereas the narrator had identified them only as "toll-collectors and *others*."[15] The word "sinners," then, is introduced by Jesus' opponents (cf. 7:34, 39; 15:2); Jesus borrows the word subsequently, but turns it on its head, as if to say, "You may call these people 'sinners,' but people like Levi are precisely those to whom I have come to extend the call to discipleship."

---

[14] James D. G. Dunn, "Pharisees, Sinners, and Jesus," in *The Social World of Formative Christianity and Judaism: Essays in Tribute to Howard Clark Kee*, ed. Jacob Neusner *et al.* (Philadelphia: Fortress, 1988) 264–89 (275–80).

[15] John Nolland suggests Luke substitutes "others" for Mark's "sinners" because "others" must now include Jesus' disciples (*Luke*, 3 vols., WBC 35 [Dallas, Texas: Word, 1989–93] 1:245), but this does not explain the introduction of "sinners" in vv. 30, 32.

Again, but now in the case of Zacchaeus, Luke reports the shock of the people at Jesus' willingness to eat with a toll-collector and sinner. But Zacchaeus does not fit the expected profile. In fact, this is a topsy-turvy tale in many respects. In chs. 1–18, Luke has portrayed people with money and power in a negative light, though in their own social world they would have been the recipients of honor and respect. Toll-collectors, on the other hand, though despised in their social world, are presented positively in Luke's narrative. How can Zacchaeus be both a toll-collector (= positive portrayal in Luke) and wealthy (= negative portrayal in Luke)? Although Zacchaeus is "wealthy," he does not fit the profile we have come to associate with the rich in Luke's Gospel; he does not enjoy relationships of reciprocity among the respectable of his community, nor does he find in his wealth a source of security apart from God. The chief characteristic of Zacchaeus is not that he is wealthy but that he is a social outcast who is willing to put his money in the service of the needy through his generosity. Hence, the previously excluded Zacchaeus is restored to the community of Israel as a son of Abraham. In a paradoxical way befitting Luke's portrayal of salvation-as-status transposition, Jesus' encounter with Zacchaeus is a proclamation of good news to the poor.

The topsy-turvy portraits we have just seen tied so fundamentally into Jesus' sense of vocation are also well integrated into his message throughout the Gospel. This is a message of salvation-as-reversal, of status transposition, of insiders becoming outsiders, of grace for unexpected people.

Jesus at the table

Luke's report of the encounters of Levi and Zacchaeus with Jesus brings to the foreground a persistent theme in the Third Gospel – namely, table fellowship. In Luke's account, not only is Jesus repeatedly at the table with the wrong people, but he also continues to attract opposition from the Jewish leadership and populace for his troublesome table companions (e.g.,

5:29–32; 7:34; 15:1–2; 19:1–10).[16] Some Lukan material portrays Jesus' table fellowship as the context in which he carried on social intercourse and teaching, as though Jesus were engaged in an eating-and-talking party like the symposia known to us via Greco-Roman literature (e.g., Luke 7:36–50; 11:37–52; 14; 22:24–27).[17] Here, though, we are more interested in the socio-religious sensibilities Jesus upset by his choice of table companions, for here we encounter in embodied form the shape of his "good news to the poor." ✓

In the ancient Mediterranean world, mealtime was a social event whose significance far outdistanced the need to satisfy one's hunger. To welcome people at the table had become tantamount to extending to them intimacy, solidarity, acceptance; table companions were treated as though they were of one's extended family. Sharing food encoded messages about hierarchy, inclusion and exclusion, boundaries and crossing boundaries.[18] Who ate with whom, where one sat in relation to whom at the table – such questions as these were charged with social meaning in the time of Jesus and Luke. As a consequence, to refuse table fellowship with people was to ostracize them, to treat them as outsiders.

It is against this backdrop that Jesus' table practices in the Third Gospel are set in sharp relief. After all, it could be argued that his detractors are the ones behaving properly. In a tension-filled environment such as Luke portrays in Palestine under Roman occupation, it was important to define loyalties carefully. Could one do so in a meal shared by some 5,000, with apparent disregard for who was sitting next to whom, for normal tests of purity (9:12–17)? In order to exercise faithfulness, should one not (as the Pharisees apparently did) emphasize practical holiness in the choice of one's food

---

[16] See Robert J. Karris, *Luke: Artist and Theologian. Luke's Passion Account as Literature*, TI (New York/Mahwah/Toronto: Paulist, 1985) esp. ch. 4; Karris' somewhat exaggerated point is that, according to Luke, Jesus got himself executed by the way he ate.

[17] See Dennis E. Smith, "Table Fellowship as a Literary Motif in the Gospel of Luke," *JBL* 106 (1987) 613–38.

[18] Mary Douglas, "Deciphering a Meal," in *Implicit Meanings: Essays in Anthropology* (London/New York: Routledge, 1975) 249–75.

and one's eating companions? Luke's account is impressive in
its realism:

> Now all the tax collectors and sinners were coming near to listen to
> Jesus. And the Pharisees and the scribes were grumbling, "This
> fellow welcomes sinners and eats with them." (Luke 15:1–2)

The point, though, is not that Jesus misunderstands the
social conventions related to eating and their religious significance. One might say that he understands them quite well,
and exploits them. The very people excluded from the table of the
holy, he welcomes, and in so doing he serves as their physician
(5:31) and extends to them salvation (19:9–10).

This is not to say that Jesus refuses table fellowship with
those of high status; this is patently not the case in Luke's
portrayal. He is found at the table of Pharisees (7:36–37;
11:37), even of a leading Pharisee (14:1). This, too, is an
embodiment of the Lukan message. The Song of Mary, it will
be recalled, celebrated the raising up of the lowly and the
bringing down of those of high status, so that both might be
able to participate fully in the purpose of God (1:46–55). Now,
in his table practices, Jesus raises up the lowly and accepts the
excluded. But he also breaks bread with those of high status,
those like Pharisees who by their attention to holiness show
themselves to be "insiders," "righteous." Will they allow their
positions of high status won by attention to religious purity to
keep them from recognizing and embracing God's purpose?

Will they refuse Jesus' invitation to sit at the table with
others, even the marginalized, to whom God has extended
grace? Will they learn to invite "the poor, the crippled, the
lame, and the blind" to their dinner parties (14:13; cf. 14:21)?
The clever juxtaposition of the grumbling Pharisees and scribes
with the elder brother of Jesus' parable of the lost son (15:1–2,
25–32) suggests that, at the time Luke was writing, the jury is
still out. What is more, the accentuated concern with table
fellowship between Jewish and Gentile believers in Acts (cf.
Acts 10:1–11:18) reveals that Luke was not only concerned
with the potential responses of Pharisees within the Gospel, but
also with the possibility of open fellowship across ethnic and

religious lines in his own time.[19] Will those who follow Jesus learn to embody the message of his scandalous table practices?

Jesus and the marginalized *sickness associated c̄ sin.*

This scandalous message is evidenced in other aspects of Jesus' ministry, too. Following through his announced program to attend the sick (5:31), Jesus in fact serves as healer to the sick – those who by demonic possession, accident of birth, sin, or whatever cause, lack physical wholeness (e.g., 4:33–36, 40–41; 5:17–26; 6:6–10, 18–19; 8:26–39, 40–56; 11:14; 13:10–17). The sick are made well. Those oppressed by evil spirits are set free. Lepers are cleansed (5:12–16; 17:11–19). The dead are raised (7:11–17; 8:40–42, 49–56). Even a slave, and that of a centurion, is not too lowly to be healed by Jesus (7:1–10).

In Jesus' ministry, sinners are accepted (5:1–11, 29–32). Children, too, who occupied a low status indeed in the Roman world, were welcomed by Jesus (18:15–17). Even Samaritans – whose comprehensive rejection of Jerusalem as the locus of Yahweh's presence and activity isolated them even from the varieties of Judaism in the first century – are not outside of the reach of Jesus' mission. A Samaritan is portrayed by Jesus at the expense of a priest and Levite as the one who loved his neighbor as he loved himself (10:25–37). And Luke narrates the healing of ten lepers in 17:11–19, noting emphatically that the only one of the ten who returned to give praise to God was a Samaritan, a foreigner (17:16, 18).

If Luke presents God's purpose as the extension of salvation in all of its fullness to all people, what of the Gentiles? Luke brackets his Gospel with references to the inclusion of Gentiles in God's people (2:30–32; 24:47; cf. Acts 1:8). However, this concern is not highlighted much in the ministry of Jesus himself. He draws an analogy between himself and the prophets Elijah and Elisha, and specifically to their ministries

[19] Cf. Philip Francis Esler, *Community and Gospel in Luke–Acts: The Social and Political Motivations of Lucan Theology*, SNTSMS 57 (Cambridge University Press, 1987) ch. 4.

among non-Jews,[20] but upon departing from Nazareth he goes not to the Gentiles but to the (Jewish) synagogue in Capernaum (4:16–37). Jesus heals the slave of a Gentile centurion, even making of this Gentile a model of faith (7:1–10). He crosses over the Sea of Galilee, *possibly* into Gentile territory,[21] to minister to a demoniac. And Luke reports that a centurion, again a Gentile, confesses Jesus as the Righteous One at Jesus' death (23:47; cf. Acts 3:13–14). Generally, though, the inclusion of the Gentiles is a matter of future significance, predicted by Simeon (2:30–32) and by Jesus (13:22–30). Jesus' primary task in the fulfillment of this aspect of God's purpose is apparently to pave the way for its achievement by his work at dissolving the barriers that separate people – Jew and Samaritan, adults and children, men and women, sick and well, righteous and sinner, and so on.

In a wide variety of ways the overarching theme of salvation-as-reversal is narrated repeatedly in the Third Gospel. We have noted some of them, and may conclude this section with three additional, suggestive examples. In 7:36–50 we are treated to an impressive inversion of normal expectations. Simon, a Pharisee, clearly assuming Jesus to be a person concerned, as Simon was, with religious purity,[22] invited Jesus to a meal. A woman, a sinner, recognizing that Jesus was "a friend of sinners" (7:34), interrupted the table scene so as to express her gratitude to Jesus. Simon, as host, should have performed normal acts of greeting when receiving Jesus into his house. He failed to do so, but the sinful woman, an outsider on whom was placed no such social expectations, performed these very tasks (7:44–46). In the end, she, not he, is the one who has received forgiveness, salvation, peace (7:47–50).

Second, Jesus tells the story in 16:19–31 of two men whose lives and fates are as closely paralleled as they are intertwined. The one is rich, is dressed in purple and fine linen, and feasts

---

[20] Note that in addition to being non-Jews, those to whom Elijah and Elisha minister are, respectively, a widow and a leper; that is, they are doubly outsiders.

[21] This is not highlighted in Luke; cf. Mark 5:1–20

[22] Given the Pharisaic concern with holiness at the table, on what other basis could Simon initiate this invitation? See also 7:39.

extravagantly on a daily basis. The other is poor, is covered with sores, and longs to eat the scraps that fall from the overflowing table of the wealthy man. The wealthy man dies and is buried – and that in a society where burial is important for all but especially for those of lofty status. The poor man dies and, in receiving no burial, is shamed even in death. In life, the wealthy man and the poor were separated by the gate to the rich man's estate. After death, they are still separated, now by a great chasm, but the wealthy man is on the wrong side. The poor man, who has a name even in life, Lazarus, is carried by angels to Abraham. But the wealthy man, who is given no name, is tormented in Hades. Abraham comments to the wealthy man, "Child, remember when you were alive you received good things; Lazarus likewise received bad things. Now, however, he is comforted here and you are in agony" (16:25). One might hear echoing in the background Jesus' own words in the Sermon on the Plain, "Blessed are you who weep now, for you will laugh ... Woe to you who are laughing now, for you will mourn and weep" (6:21, 25).

Finally, Jesus tells the story of a Pharisee and a toll-collector (18:9–14). Both go up to the temple to pray and, as in 16:19–31, these two are portrayed as opposites. One rejoices in his piety, the other mourns in his sinfulness. Jesus remarks that it is the toll-collector who goes home justified, "for all who exalt themselves will be humbled, but all who humble themselves will be exalted" (18:14).

"Behold, some are last who will be first, and some are first who will be last" (13:30).[23]

Jesus and women

The status of women in Roman antiquity also marks this population group as living on the margins, but because of the particular attention given to women in the Third Gospel, we will explore their portrayal separately.

---

[23] Cf. John O. York. *The Last Shall Be First: The Rhetoric of Reversal in Luke,* JSNTSS 46 (Sheffield: JSOT, 1991).

When in 4:16–30 Jesus lays out the shape of his mission, he does so, in part, by drawing a typological relationship between himself and Elijah (4:25–26; cf. 1 Kgs. 17:8–24). Luke's primary concern here is not to announce proleptically the rejection of Israel, a factor not mentioned in the Elijah material Luke borrows, but rather to add to Luke's characterization of Jesus' identity and mission.[24] Interestingly, the episode Luke uses to draw out this analogy concerns a person whose status as an outsider is heavily emphasized. The person to whom Elijah is sent is (1) a non-Jew, (2) a woman, and (3) a widow – a person of the lowest status who, according to the Scriptures, is to be the object of special concern (e.g., Exod. 22:22; Deut. 10:18; 24:19–21). Luke narrates an episode in the life of Jesus that closely resembles the Elijah-story, showing Jesus' own embodiment of this concern (7:11–17). Elsewhere, a widow receives justice (18:1–8) and so becomes a symbol of God's chosen ones. The poor widow who gives two small copper coins to the temple treasury may serve as a model of exemplary piety (21:1–4); in light of the immediately preceding critique of Jewish leaders who devour the homes of widows (20:45–47), however, it is more likely that we should read Jesus' remarks about the widow in the temple as an indictment against a system that has resulted in the victimization of this woman who, in giving everything, has lost even the roof over her head.

Luke 4:25–27 brings to the fore a second interest of the Third Evangelist. Here Luke places in parallel the widow at Zarephath and Naaman the Syrian, just as throughout the Third Gospel he devises female–male parallelism.[25]

Zechariah and Mary	1:10–20, 26–38
Simeon and Anna	2:25–38
healing of demoniac and of Simon's mother-in-law	4:31–39
centurion and widow	7:1–17

---

[24] See Robert L. Brawley, *Luke–Acts and the Jews: Conflict, Apology, and Conciliation*, SBLMS 33 (Atlanta, Georgia: Scholars, 1987) 6–27.

[25] For additional possibilities, see, e.g., Mary Rose D'Angelo, "Women in Luke–Acts: A Redactional View," *JBL* 109 (1990) 441–61 (443–46).

man with mustard seed and woman with leaven	13:18–21
woman-bent-over and man with dropsy	13:10–17; 14:1–6
man with 100 sheep and woman with 10 silver coins	15:4–10

This emphasis comes as no real surprise to readers of Luke's birth narratives. Already there God's grace had been evident in the care given to Elizabeth (shamed in her childlessness – 1:25, 58) and Mary (on whom God had looked with favor – 1:28, 30, 48), just as these two women stood out in the opening chapter (in contrast to a male priest) for their open-handed responses to God's activity. Elsewhere, women in the Third Gospel appear as recipients of healing (4:38–39; 8:2, 40–56; 13:10–17), exemplars of faith and faithfulness (7:36–50; 8:42b–48; 18:1–8; 24:1–10), and as Jesus' traveling companions and benefactors (8:1–3). In the birth narrative, Mary and Elizabeth are presented as spokespersons for God who interpret, especially for Luke's readers, the significance of the coming of John and Jesus into the world (1:42–55). In the same way, Anna spoke of the child to those awaiting the redemption of Jerusalem (2:38). In the resurrection narrative, it is women who see the empty tomb, hear the angelic message, remember the words of Jesus, and speak of all of this to Jesus' followers. Again, their faithful witness is set in contrast to the response of the male disciples, who regard their news as only idle talk (24:11) until it is confirmed by other men (24:34–35).

This portrait is significant for the degree to which it contrasts with what we know of women in Greco-Roman antiquity in general. This was a patriarchal world, with women, as a whole, held in low esteem. Of course, there were exceptions to the over-all negative picture; one may point to evidence that some women held the office of synagogue ruler in ancient Judaism and of priest in Roman religion, or to the wider role of women in business and benefaction in the Roman world.[26] Even after

---

[26] Cf., e.g., Bernadette J. Brooten, *Women Leaders in the Ancient Synagogue*, BJS 36 (Atlanta, Georgia: Scholars, 1982); Ben Witherington III, *Women in the Earliest Churches*, SNTSMS 59 (Cambridge University Press, 1988) ch. 1.

this is considered, however, the degree to which Luke speaks of
women at all is surely of consequence. What may be of even
greater consequence, though, is the way issues of status, including those related to gender and sex, have been criticized and
undercut more broadly in the Third Gospel. The reorientation
of status-definition and characterization of salvation as status-
inversion proposed in Luke had, already in the fact of its
proposal, managed to break free from the cultural moorings of
Greco-Roman antiquity.

SALVATION AND ESCHATOLOGY

Luke uses the language of salvation more than any other New
Testament writer,[27] but employs that language in co-texts
whose effect is to give salvation broad meaning. Salvation is,
preeminently, status reversal, and this includes not only the
raising up of lowly persons whom Jesus encounters in the
Gospel, but also the people of Israel as a people, promised
liberation from the oppressive hand of Rome. Salvation is also
the coming of the kingdom of God, then, the coming of God's
reign of justice, to deconstruct the worldly systems and values
at odds with the purpose of God. Salvation also entails membership in the new community God is drawing together around
Jesus, a community into which all – especially the previously
excluded for reasons of sin, and its corollary, despised status –
are invited to participate in the blessings of the kingdom as well
as to share in its service. If this begins to lay out the nature of
salvation, the question remains, when? When is this salvation
available?

Without a doubt, the Lukan emphasis falls above all on
salvation in the present. "*Today!*" he announces at Nazareth,
"this Scripture has been fulfilled in your hearing" (4:21), just
as he proclaims to Zacchaeus, "*Today* salvation has come to
this house ..." (19:9). To the Pharisees he remarks that if he
casts out demons by the power ("finger") of God, then the

---

27 Σῴζω ("to save") – 6:9; 7:50; 8:12, 36, 48, 50; 9:24 (2x); 13:23; 17:19; 18:26, 42;
    19:10; 23:35 (2x), 39; σωτήρ ("savior") – 1:47; 2:11; σωτηρία ("salvation") – 1:69,
    71, 77; 19:9; σωτήριον ("salvation") – 2:30; 3:6.

kingdom of God has already come (11:20). Asked about the timing of the kingdom, Jesus replies, "The kingdom of God is in your midst!" (17:21).[28]

Jesus the healer

The Lukan sketch of Jesus as healer is significant not only for its emphasis on Jesus' concern for those in greatest need, but also for its importance in our understanding of the Lukan eschatology. In his ministry of healing, Jesus provides concrete evidence for the presence of the in-breaking kingdom of God.

Luke 4:18–19 anticipate the healing role of Jesus, a role that will be realized within the narrative almost immediately at Capernaum – in the synagogue and in a home (4:31–39). In this way, Jesus' healing ministry is explicated as integral to God's saving purpose and thus to Jesus' announcement of good news. This interpretation is not lost on the Galilean crowds. They see in Jesus' ability to raise a dead man to life the coming of the eschatological prophet, the gracious intervention of God to bring salvation (7:16).

John, who had anticipated messianic judgment (3:7, 16–17) and not a ministry of compassion, is not so sure. Is this ministry of healing the sick, this care for the needy, really indicative of the messianic age? Could Jesus really be the Coming One, the Messiah? Jesus' answer echoes his earlier summation of his ministry in 4:18–19, itself based on Isa. 58:6; 61:1–2:

At that moment Jesus healed many people of their diseases, plagues, and evil spirits, and he gave sight to many who were blind. And he said to [John's disciples], "Go, tell John what you have seen and heard: the blind receive their sight, the lame walk, lepers are cleansed, the deaf hear, the dead are raised, and the poor have good news brought to them." (7:21–22)

Jesus' words and deeds signal that he is the One for whom John had prepared. As evidence, Jesus gives his ministry of healing. By means of its intertextual relationship to 4:18–19, this

---

[28] The Greek phrase, ἐντὸς ὑμῶν ἐστιν, has been rendered by some as "is in you," taking the kingdom more as a spiritual reality (e.g., TEV, NIV). However, this

episode is rooted deeply in the eschatological vision of Isaiah, indicating that Jesus understood his healing and exorcisms not simply as "bringing good news to the poor," but as inaugurating the long-awaited epoch of salvation. Similarly, when instructing his disciples as he sends them out on their own mission, he draws an equation between healing and announcing the drawing near of the kingdom of God (10:9, 11).

When it is recognized that for Luke (almost?) all diseases are expressions of evil, it is not surprising that healing is regarded as a vital sign of the new era. In 13:12, 15–16, the language of binding and loosing directly relates the healing of the woman bent over to her having been released from the bondage of Satan. Jesus rebukes the fever of Simon's mother-in-law (4:38–39), just as he rebukes demons (4:41). In a retrospective summary of Jesus' ministry, Peter reiterates how Jesus "healed all who were under the power of the devil" (Acts 10:38). The mural Luke paints highlights the cosmic forces engaged in Jesus' ministry. Luke narrates the conflict between two worlds, the world over which the devil claims sovereignty (4:6) and the new world of God's reign.[29]

This healing effected in Jesus' ministry brought to present experience the promise of eschatological redemption. Healing for Luke, then, was always more than a physical experience, just as disease was always experienced as more than a physical malady. Within the world Luke portrays, reports about sick people have to do with physical misfortune *and* its social consequences. Hence, to be sick was to be in need of personal, physical benefit, but also of more holistic healing.

The woman who suffered a hemorrhage, for example, had a physical malady, but not a life-threatening one; after all, she had been suffering for twelve years (8:43–48). Her problem was public, though, well known in her community as a con-

makes no sense of the plural form of the pronoun "you"; of the ambivalent, largely skeptical characterization of the Pharisees thus far; or of the larger Lukan portrait of the nature of the kingdom as a religio-social reality.

29 See Howard Clark Kee, *Miracle in the Early Christian World: A Study in Sociohistorical Method* (New Haven/London: Yale University Press, 1983) 204: "From the cosmic perspective, Jesus' healings and exorcisms were regarded by Luke as essential factors in the defeat of the God-opposing powers."

sequence of her unhappy experience with physicians who had taken her money but had not helped her. Her predicament in the end was less physical than social, for she lived in a constant state of impurity, thus isolated from her community.[30] Jesus' pronouncement of well-being and shalom (8:48) must be understood as connoting physical healing, then (cf. 8:44), but also as restoration to the community of Israel.

Likewise, the account of the restoration of a dead man in 7:11–17 is in reality much less about the dead man and much more about his mother. Note how Luke describes the dead man: "he was his mother's only son." Add to this the further comment that "she was a widow" and we begin to understand why "Jesus had compassion *on her*" (not "on the dead man"). With the death of her son, this widow was reduced to a state of desperate vulnerability; hence, after raising the dead man, "Jesus gave him to his mother." The same may be said of the Gerasene demoniac – at first alone, out of control, naked, demon-possessed; then sitting, clothed, in his right mind, and instructed by Jesus to return home to his community (8:26–39). Or in 13:10–17 a woman is recognized by Jesus as a "daughter of Abraham" – previously bent over by disease, excluded by her shame in the community, now restored to the community of God's people. Again, salvation is represented in concrete terms – refusing any boundaries between social/communal, material/physical, and spiritual/religious – and in the present by Jesus' ministry of healing.

The parousia of Jesus

Luke's emphasis on salvation in the present led Conzelmann to believe that Luke had substituted a theory of the progress of the church in history for the earlier Christian hope in the impending parousia, or return of Jesus.[31] In fact, Luke's presentation

---

[30] See Lev. 15:19–31; 11QTemple 48:14–17; *m. Niddah*. What is more, on account of her attempts to find treatment, she had been reduced to poverty (8:43).

[31] Hans Conzelmann, *The Theology of St. Luke* (London: Faber and Faber, 1960). On the question of Lukan eschatology, see John T. Carroll, *Response to the End of History: Eschatology and Situation in Luke–Acts*, SBLDS 92 (Atlanta, Georgia: Scholars, 1988);

of the timing of the return of the Son of Man is more variegated. The end is very near, at hand, according to some texts
(18:7–8; 21:31–32). According to others, a delay seems to be
envisioned (12:45; 19:11). Two points are implied here. First,
Luke has not simply collapsed the eschatological hope of salvation into the present; the kingdom of God has a future
element as well as a present one. Second, Luke's presentation of
the parousia defies oversimplification; as regards its timing, "it
is not for you to know" (Acts 1:7). These two points can be
developed further.

First, Gabriel, Mary, Zechariah, John, and finally Jesus,
speaking on behalf of God, make wide-ranging promises about
the extent of the salvation being proffered by God. Spiritual,
material, social, and political deliverance is promised, including the restoration of Israel. Of course, our understanding of
the liberation envisioned by, say, the Song of Zechariah
(1:68–79) depends in large part on how we evaluate the needs
represented by the Song. Painting the picture of first-century
Palestine with images of a grossly oppressive militaristic,
economic, and political foreign presence will lead us to read in
Zechariah's Song the expression of deep-seated revolutionary
hopes held by a people thrust violently to the margins of
society.[32] A much less desperate portrayal, one which emphasizes the need both to recognize the difficulties of alien domination and to place those within the wider perspective of
common (especially peasant) life in antiquity,[33] orients
"deliverance" less along militaristic-revolutionary lines and
more in terms of socio-religious power. This whole problem is
further exacerbated by three other factors. First, the Jewish
people of Roman Palestine responded to their life circum-

Hans F. Bayer, "Christ-Centered Eschatology in Acts 3:17–26," in *Jesus of
Nazareth: Lord and Christ*, ed. Joel B. Green and Max Turner (Grand Rapids,
Michigan: Wm. B. Eerdmans, 1994) 236–50.

[32] See, e.g., J. Massyngbaerde Ford, *My Enemy Is My Guest: Jesus and Violence in Luke*
(Maryknoll, New York: Orbis, 1984) chs. 1–2; Richard Horsley, *The Liberation of
Christmas: The Infancy Narratives in Social Context* (New York: Crossroad, 1989)
114–19. Cf. Horsley, *Jesus and the Spiral of Violence: Popular Jewish Resistance in Roman
Palestine* (San Francisco: Harper & Row, 1987).

[33] Cf. E. P. Sanders, *Judaism: Practice and Belief, 63 BCE–66 CE* (London: SCM; Philadelphia: Trinity, 1992) e.g. 146–69.

stances in a variety of ways, so that "deliverance" might have
been defined in a variety of ways. Second, the language of
Zechariah's Song (e.g., "enemies," "those who hate us") is
highly stylized and it is not immediately clear how literally
such terms are to be read. Third, in Luke's own discourse
situation, presumably a more-or-less different set of issues
would have been brought to the surface by this language of
salvation. That is, in the larger Greco-Roman world of Luke,
"enemies" might have appeared in faces other than those of the
Roman soldier or toll-collector; cosmic and rapidly evolving
cultural forces threatened life in other ways.

Without denying the possibility, even desirability of such an
expansion of referents, the central question we must ask is, how
has the narrative taught us to read this language?[34] The
obvious point of entry for dealing with this issue is the preceding material, which opens with reference to the overlordship of Rome (1:5) and goes on to emphasize inequities of
power and wealth requiring divine attention. At the same
time, in terms of narrative development, (a) Zechariah's Song
is not the last word for our understanding of the nature of
anticipated redemption, for the narrative continues to develop,
even reshape, those expectations; and (b) the narrative of
Luke–Acts as a whole is open-ended for the story it narrates,
the consummation of God's purpose, is not completed. Hence,
room must be left for a fulfillment of expectations outside (or
beyond) the narrative as well as a reshaping of those expectations actually supported by the narrative as a whole. One need
not speak of a failure of hope because the far-reaching vision of
salvation highlighted by Luke is not achieved by the close of
Luke–Acts; the story of God's purpose is still being written as
we await the promised end.

At the same time, it is worth reflecting on the nature of the
end as Luke portrays it. One of the most astounding images we
are given is not one of violent overthrow but of the consum-

---

[34] In other words, even though one may find in the deliverance of which Zechariah
   speaks a meaningful basis for salvific hope not directly related to Zechariah's story,
   the temptation to neglect meaning in the text must be avoided. Otherwise, the
   Lukan narrative loses its power to challenge and shape understanding.

mation of the inversion of status and values propagated by
Jesus throughout his ministry in the Third Gospel (12:35–38).
The words are chosen carefully: the master will sit his faithful
slaves at the table to eat, and he (the master) will serve them
(the slaves). In this carefully constructed picture, we find
resonances of the intimacy and solidarity of table fellowship
and the transposition of roles (masters serving slaves?) already
at work in Jesus' ministry. In short, "the end" will be nothing
more or less than the completion of the work Jesus had already
begun, the consummation of God's redemptive purpose.

Second, of course, this Lukan emphasis is not made at the
expense of the motif of judgment, anticipated by John
(3:16–17) and furthered by Jesus (e.g., 12:46, 48; 17:28–30;
19:27). But the motif of judgment is developed in Jesus' eschatological discourses in the service of a larger topos – namely,
the necessity of alertness: "That slave who knew what his
master wanted, but did not prepare himself or do what was
wanted, will receive a severe beating" (12:47). We move, then,
to our second point related to the timing of the parousia.

The chronology of the end is subject to divine prerogative
and cannot be determined or known by anyone else (cf.
12:35–38); the kingdom of God is a gift (12:32), not an entity
that can be fabricated or whose timing can be determined by
humans. The end is certain to come, but with respect to its
timing, Luke counsels agnosticism. This "not knowing" is not
an occasion for laxness with regard to pursuing the divine aim,
however. Luke may have witnessed a loss of urgency in mission
activity (cf. Acts 1:6–11), complacency in the execution of
appointed responsibilities (cf. 12:35–48), and a "business as
usual" attitude toward life (cf. 17:26–30) that no longer reck-
oned with Jesus' return. In this case, Luke's emphasis on the
certainty but unpredictability of the parousia would have
underscored the significance of the future for present faithfulness.[35]

In this way, Luke characterizes the shape of the mission for
which Jesus was anointed, the sort of people to whom he was

[35] So Carroll, *Response to the End of History*, 166.

sent, and the nature of the divine purpose he would serve and, in time, bring to consummation. In this way, Luke also identifies the present as the arena in which those who follow Jesus must follow him in mission on behalf of the poor, the disadvantaged, the sick, the lost – that is, on behalf of the redemptive aim of God.

CHAPTER 5

"Let them take up the cross daily":
the way of discipleship

It is not until Luke's second volume, the Acts of the Apostles, that the disciples of Jesus come into their own as significant characters in the narrative of Christian beginnings. Their role in the Third Gospel is more passive, with the spotlight rarely leaving Jesus once he enters upon his public ministry. This is not to say the activity of the disciples in Acts is unanticipated. In his retrospective summary of the Third Gospel the disciples are mentioned for their having been chosen and instructed by Jesus (Acts 1:2). Luke understands the disciples primarily as the recipients of Jesus' training until they are commissioned to continue his work (22:28–30; 24:47).

One of the ways Luke helps to build a bridge between his two volumes on the subject of discipleship is with the prominence in Acts of "the Way" as a description of the community of Jesus' followers and its teaching (Acts 9:2; 19:9, 23; 22:4; 24:14, 22). In Acts "the Way" designates a people who align themselves with and serve God's plan, especially as witnessed in the Scriptures and manifest in Jesus (cf. Acts 18:24–25; cf., e.g., Luke 1:6; 20:21). This usage is rooted already in the Gospel of Luke – both in its utilization of the term "way" (ὁδός) and in the attention it otherwise gives to the journey motif. Drawing on Isaianic material, the narrative shows that John's role is to prepare the way of the Lord (1:76; 3:4–5; cf. 7:27; Isa. 40:3–4; Mal. 3:1), so that he (i.e. Jesus, already identified as "Lord" in 1:43) might "guide our feet in the way of peace" (1:79; cf. Isa. 59:8). More pervasive than such echoes as these, though, is the emphasis on the formation of disciples on the way.

This journey motif is especially transparent at the end of the Gospel, in 24:13–35. Two disciples were making their way to Emmaus (24:13), talking about what had happened in Jerusalem; Jesus joins them on their journey (24:15) and asks them what they were discussing as they walked along the road (24:17); Jesus travels with them to Emmaus, instructing them in the Scriptures (24:27); having come to recognize Jesus, the disciples remark, "Weren't our hearts burning within us while he was talking to us on the road, while he was opening the Scriptures to us?" (24:32); later, these two report to the other disciples "what had happened on the road" (24:35). Readers of Luke may be reminded of the longer journey in the center of the Gospel, stretching from 9:51–19:27, on which Jesus teaches his disciples on the way to Jerusalem.[1]

Prior to the time when Jesus "set his face to go to Jerusalem" (9:51), the disciples have little to add to Luke's narrative. "Disciples" appear in 5:30, 33; 6:1, but as little more than stage props. Jesus calls his disciples to him in 6:13 so that he can choose from among them twelve apostles, but he gives them no responsibilities.[2] They are simply "with him" (6:17; 8:22; cf. 8:1; 9:10; 22:11, 14, 39) and receive instruction along with the crowds (6:17, 20; 7:1). As the turning-point in the narrative, the shift from Galilean itinerancy to the Jerusalem journey, looms closer, the disciples begin to appear more often and in more active roles. They do not understand Jesus' identity, and so respond with fear and amazement when he calms the wind and water on a boat trip (8:22–25). Yet Jesus entrusts them with power and authority to heal and proclaim the kingdom of God (9:1–9).

In spite of the disciples' success (9:6), however, like Herod (9:7–9) they fail still to grasp his identity, with the result that they want to send away the hungry crowds rather than exercise faith in Jesus' ability to provide for them (9:12–17). The size of the crowd (5,000) is matched only by the quantity of food left

---

[1] Arthur A. Just Jr., *The Ongoing Feast: Table Fellowship and Eschatology at Emmaus* (Collegeville, Minnesota: Liturgical, 1993) 58.

[2] Cf. Mark 3:14–15: "he appointed twelve ... to be with him, and to be sent out to proclaim the message and to have authority to exorcise demons."

over after the meal, twelve baskets, one for each disciple (9:17).
Jesus' feeding miracle and subsequent prayer are effective for
preparing for Peter's confession of Jesus as "The Messiah of
God" (9:18–20).

As important and positive a confession as this might be, it is
clearly not enough. The possibility of the failure of the disciples
was raised already in 6:16, with the identification of Judas as a
traitor. This possibility is now realized to some extent by all of
the twelve: they continue to misunderstand (9:33), fail to
appropriate the power of the Lord on behalf of a possessed
child (9:37–41), and even engage in internal debate over which
among them is the greatest (9:46). Their misapprehension is
somehow related to their failure to account fully for Jesus'
impending suffering and death (9:21–27, 44–45). And, in fact,
Jesus announces that the disciples, too, must take up their cross
day-by-day (9:23; cf. 14:27). As the Jerusalem journey begins,
the relationship between Jesus and his disciples is at a low ebb
indeed.

It is true that the journey of Jesus and his followers to
Jerusalem is not straightforward. They meander, making little
or no progress toward their destination, and few geographical
markers are provided to signal what progress is made. Nevertheless, reminders of the journey punctuate this whole central
section of Luke's Gospel (e.g., 9:51; 10:38; 13:22, 33; 14:25;
17:11), with their frequency increasing as Jerusalem looms
larger on the horizon (18:31, 35; 19:1, 11). Two motifs are
outstanding in this journey. First, Luke emphasizes its destination – Jerusalem, the site of Jesus' "exodus" (9:31, 51). By
this expression Luke refers to "Jesus' pathway through death to
exaltation at the right hand of God"[3] – that is, Jesus' aim is to
fulfill the purpose of God for which he was sent and to which he
has committed himself.

Second, 9:51–19:27 is overwhelmingly didactic in content;
only 9:51–56; 11:14–16; 13:10–13; 14:1–6; 17:11–19; and

---

[3] John Nolland, *Luke*, 3 vols., WBC 35 (Dallas, Texas: Word, 1989–93) II:535; cf.
Gerhard Schneider, *Das Evangelium Lukas*, 2nd ed., OTKNT 3.1 (Gütersloh: Gerd
Mohn; Würtzburg: Echter, 1984) I:229. It is not clear how else one is otherwise to
make sense of τὰς ἡμέρας ("days"; cf. Acts 1:2, 22: "day") in 9:51.

18:35–43 contain material other than sayings. The disciples appear more often in this section than elsewhere in the Gospel, often receiving instruction (10:23; 11:1; 12:1, 22; 16:1; 17:1, 5, 22; 18:15, 31). This is not in every case private instruction (cf. 10:23); for example, in 16:1–31, even when we are told explicitly that Jesus is addressing the disciples, we learn that Pharisees were eavesdropping (16:14). Similarly, the dual presence of disciples and crowds in ch. 12 leads Peter to ask Jesus to whom his end-time parable was being addressed – "to us or to everyone?" (12:41). As with the presentation of the Sermon on the Plain (6:17; 7:1), then, the line between disciples and others is not always sharply drawn (cf. 9:49–50). Jesus gives positive instruction and warnings on the way of discipleship that serve also as a challenge and invitation to prospective followers. Luke thus makes use of the journey motif to solidify the relation between disciples and master, to provide instruction on the way of discipleship, and to encourage people to join him on the journey of serving God's purpose.

BEGINNING THE JOURNEY

According to Luke, how does one enter the journey of discipleship? Two factors complicate how one might address this question. First, the point at which one has joined the journey is not always clear in Luke. In some cases a clear "call to discipleship" and/or conversion is offered (e.g., 5:1–11), but in others persons previously unknown to us respond as though they have already been on the journey (e.g., 7:1–10, 36–50; 8:43–48). No doubt, part of this ambiguity arises from the very boundaries between "us" and "them" that Jesus works to dissolve. How could a Gentile centurion or an unclean woman already have begun to orient life around the way of the Lord? According to normal conventions, the very conventions Jesus works to overturn, such people are by definition far from the "way of the Lord." Second, no two encounters with Jesus are exactly the same; Luke has not taken it upon himself to smooth his various accounts of disciple-calling into a standard format. This is the beauty of "story" – its ability to present with realism something of the ambiguity of life as it is lived, its capacity to show the rich interrelatedness of forces that shape human experience in concrete situations. This is also the challenge of "story," for this type of communication works against systematic treatment.[4] What we can do, then, is articulate a number of recurring motifs that are suggestive of how one becomes active in the way of discipleship.

The initiative of Jesus

In the broadest sense, discipleship is possible at all because of the gracious intervention of God in human affairs. More narrowly, Luke portrays Jesus as going to people and calling them to join him in discipleship (5:1–11, 27; 9:59; 18:22). Compared to the portrayal of disciple-calling in the Gospel of Mark, Luke's understanding is less spectacular. In Mark, Jesus issues his command, "Follow me!", without warning, with no previous interaction. Luke, on the other hand, locates the call to discipleship more fully in the context of Jesus' ongoing mission in an area. It is after having already healed Simon's mother-in-law (4:38–39) and instructing Simon in his vocation as a fisherman that Jesus heralds Simon's change of vocation: "From now on you will be catching people!" (5:1–11).

Jesus' initiative is nonetheless arresting in its inclusiveness. He crosses socio-religious boundaries to call a self-proclaimed "sinner" (5:8) and a toll-collector (5:27), and even counts women among his disciples (8:2–3).

Faith

In Acts, the response of faith becomes an explicit requirement for salvation (e.g., Acts 16:31). Although not so prominent in the Third Gospel, faith is nevertheless a hallmark of proper response to God's work in Jesus. The devil may take away the word so that people might not believe and be saved (8:12).

---

[4] See Eduard Schweizer, *Luke: A Challenge to Present Theology* (London: SPCK; Atlanta, Georgia: John Knox, 1982) 60–61.

Likewise, in 8:50 faith is indicated as a precursor to salvation (cf. 5:20; 7:9, 47–50; 8:48; 17:19; 18:42). Especially because of the danger of apostasy (cf. 8:12), faith is an ongoing need for those on the way of discipleship. Particularly acute is the need for a proper recognition of Jesus' identity and concomitant faith in his ability to provide for one's needs (8:25; 12:22–34; 16:5–6); and for "faithfulness" – that is, persistence on the journey (e.g., 8:13–14; 18:1–8).

Repentance

Repentance (along with "turning") is a key term describing one's proper response to the offer of salvation in Acts (e.g., Acts 2:38; 3:19; 5:31; 8:22), but as a term it is not often found in the Third Gospel. The *concept* of repentance is present everywhere in the Gospel of Luke, however, and has to do above all with the redirection of one's heart and life toward the purpose of God. Images of repentance abound – for example, in the account of would-be disciples who refuse to so re-orient their lives (9:57–62), in the parable of the lost son who came to his senses and returned to his father's house (15:11–32), and in the scene of the execution where the crowds "returned home, beating their breasts" (23:48).

"Repentance" gains its first meaning in the Lukan narrative in the account of John's ministry (3:1–14). Having heard him proclaim a baptism of repentance, the crowds ask, "What then should we do?" This is followed by similar questions from toll-collectors and soldiers. John's answers – give your extra clothing and food to those in need, etc. – concretize "repentance" in terms of everyday life. His baptism is thus seen as an initiatory rite of passage by which people embrace the challenge to reflect in their lives ways of living appropriate to true children of Abraham. John's answers to the crowds, the toll-collectors, and soldiers reach into the realities of day-to-day existence.

Against this backdrop, it is not surprising to find Jesus' disciples leaving everything to follow Jesus (5:11, 28). Indeed, Jesus asserts, "None of you can become my disciple if you do not give up all your possessions" (14:33; 18:22, 28); this is a corollary of faith and reception of the gift of God's kingdom (12:32–34). Even family ties may be forfeited in light of the absolute claims of the kingdom of God (9:59–60; 12:52–53; 14:26; but cf. 8:39).

Repentance entails re-directing one's life so as to serve only one master, God (16:13), and this demands allegiance in all things. This is why Luke locates Jesus' question, "Why do you call me 'Lord, Lord,' and do not do what I tell you?" (6:46) at the end of the Sermon on the Plain, so as to emphasize the importance of hearing and obeying (cf. 8:21; 10:38–42; 11:27–28). Radical obedience is the order of the day as disciples wait for the return of the Master (12:35–48; cf. 13:24–27; 17:7–10). These are new times, according to the Lukan narrative, and they demand a new level of obedience to the ancient but ever-current purpose of God (5:36–39). For this reason, Luke stresses the cost of discipleship and urges would-be disciples to count the cost before entering the journey (14:25–33).

Following Jesus

Jesus defines discipleship as following him (9:23), a concept Luke develops above all by noting the presence of the disciples continually "with" Jesus (6:17; 7:11; 8:1, 22; 9:10; 22:11, 14, 28, 39; cf. 8:38; 22:33). This may seem a rather vague and passive role, this "being with Jesus," but in Acts it becomes one of the key credentials for the apostolic office (Acts 1:21). Being with Jesus suggests companionship with Jesus, sharing in his success and failure, his acceptance and rejection; it entails identifying with and being shaped by Jesus' own life and mission.

In Luke 9:43, following Jesus is understood in the context of self-denial and daily cross-bearing. On the one hand, Luke seems to have in mind some form of impending persecution of Jesus' followers – hence, the emphasis on public denial of oneself rather than of one's faith in Jesus (cf. 9:24–26; 12:8–12). On the other, the threat of execution is apparently not present; after all, Luke's emphasis on *daily* cross-bearing precludes a literal understanding of "cross-bearing" as preparation for one's own crucifixion. Set within the context of Jesus' journey to Jerusalem, this cross-bearing must mean embracing and serving in a single-minded way (setting one's face to, 9:51) the redemptive purpose of God.

Involvement in mission

Being "with" Jesus eventually entails sharing in his missionary agenda. Although the Twelve receive no explicit assignment when they are chosen to be apostles (6:12–16), they are later sent out to proclaim the kingdom of God and to heal (9:1–2; cf. 10:1–11). In this way they begin to fulfill what was anticipated in the case of Simon and his fishing partners – "From now on you will be catching people" (5:10). In his entry into the way of discipleship Levi had already begun to participate in this "catching people," providing Jesus a setting in which to serve as physician to "the sick" (5:29–32). Eventually, Jesus will commission his chosen ones to extend his ministry to all nations (24:49).

PRAYER AND PRAISE

Recognizing that Luke knows nothing of a relationship with God that does not immediately work itself out in relationship to others,[5] we may nonetheless focus our attention momentarily on how he describes appropriate responses to the grace of God. Of course, this is already to recognize that Luke portrays God as working graciously in the world, bringing to realization the longstanding promises to God's people. For him, the new era is dawning, as represented by the fulfillment of scriptural promises, the accelerated activity of the eschatological Spirit of God, and the offer of salvation through Jesus' ministry. God has worked first, then, bringing to fruition his redemptive plan. How might humans respond? We have already mentioned such

[5] For this emphasis throughout the biblical materials, see Paul D. Hanson, *The People Called: The Growth of Community in the Bible* (San Francisco: Harper & Row, 1986).

motifs of response as repentance and faith, participation in the mission of Jesus and obedience to the Lord. We will go on to highlight more closely one's response *vis-à-vis* possessions and community life. Here we may focus more centrally on two additional responses Luke himself repeatedly emphasizes – praise and prayer.

Already dominant on the landscape of the Lukan birth narrative is joy and praise (e.g., 1:14, 28, 44, 47, 58, 64, 68; 2:10, 13, 20, 28–29, 38). This is perhaps expected in stories of childbirth, but Luke's interest transcends the happiness attending childbirth in general. In his view, these are not ordinary births; they are of eschatological importance, marking the coming of salvation, and this calls for eschatological celebration.[6] Indeed, even John, still in the womb, leaps with joy at the advent of divine redemption (1:41, 44).[7]

The saving work of Jesus is also the occasion for praise in the Third Gospel. This is particularly true of Jesus' miracles of healing, for repeatedly Luke reports that in response to a healing, the one healed and/or those present "glorified God" (e.g, 5:26; 7:16; 13:13; 18:43; cf. Acts 4:21; 11:18; 13:48; 21:20).[8] Among these occurrences of the praise-response, 7:16 is particularly telling since it appears in tandem with a further response from the crowd: "A great prophet has risen among us!" and "God has looked with favor on his people!" What Luke reports is that people recognize God's gracious visitation (cf. 1:68, 78) in the work of Jesus. This "praise," therefore, is not the mindless response of the masses, but an enlightened one. Divine deliverance is at hand, and this elicits responses of joy and praise (cf. 15:6, 9, 23–24). In an unhappy contrast, Luke observes that Jerusalem failed to recognize "the time of your visitation from God"; hence, there is no rejoicing, only tears (19:41–44).

---

6 On joy as related to the advent of salvation, see 1:44; 2:10; 10:17; Acts 2:46; *Sib. Or.* 3.619–23, 767–95.

7 On the association of "leaping" with the experience of God's salvation see Mal. 4:2; Gottfried Fitzer, "σκιρτάω" in *TDNT* 7:401–2.

8 This *theo*logical perspective is maintained throughout the Gospel with one exception. In 17:15–16, Luke indicates that the Samaritan leper, cleansed by Jesus, returns to praise God and to give grateful homage to Jesus.

Earlier we saw the importance to Luke's christology of the prayer life of Jesus. To this we may now add the importance of prayer to Luke's understanding of discipleship, presented both by Jesus' example as one who regularly prays and by the ample instruction on prayer in the Third Gospel.

An examination of the instruction on prayer in Luke reveals two major emphases – the one focusing on God, the other on the disciples. First, Jesus, who repeatedly addresses God as Father (2:49; 10:21–22; 22:42; 23:43, 46; cf. 22:29; 24:49), teaches his disciples to address God in like fashion. Indeed, his teaching on prayer in 11:2–13 begins and ends with references to God as the Father of the disciples (11:2, 13). Elsewhere, too, when addressing the disciples Jesus refers to God as "your Father" (6:36; 12:30, 32). Thus emphasized is the special relationship with God available to disciples, stressing the degree to which the distance between heaven and earth has been bridged by the fulfillment of God's redemptive activity. Coupled with this emphasis is a focus on the faithfulness of God to hear and act. In particular, Jesus counters the potential anxiety of the disciples by observing that "your Father" knows what you need (12:30). Disciples are to pray for the kingdom to come, for daily bread, and so on (12:2–4), and then to trust God to grant the gift of the kingdom and, with it, the necessities of life (12:31–32). Such faithfulness on God's part frees disciples to live without anxiety, but also to place their security in God rather than in possessions and stored wealth (12:14–21, 32–34).

According to Jesus, God's faithfulness far outdistances the goodness one might expect to receive from one's human father (11:9–13). As a consequence of prayer, God will grant the Holy Spirit. Later in Luke, this gift becomes "the promise of my Father" (24:49; cf. Acts 1:4), and, as anticipated, it is when the disciples are together in prayer that the gift of the Spirit is poured out upon them all (Acts 1:14; 2:1–4).

The motif of prayer appears in the Third Gospel by way of highlighting God's faithfulness to his children, but also to encourage Jesus' followers to replicate his fidelity in their lives. Fervent prayer, exemplified by Jesus, is advised for difficult circumstances encountered by disciples (22:40, 46). Earlier, this same steadfastness in the midst of trials had been illustrated by a widow in a parable Jesus told to the disciples "about their need to pray always and not to lose heart" (18:1–8). In the face of injustice, she did not lose heart but continued to seek help. Because God is faithful, he will hear and act; can Jesus anticipate analogous constancy on the part of his followers (18:7–8; cf. 11:5–8)?

THE ECONOMY OF THE KINGDOM

Prominent among the several motifs serving the larger theme in Luke of advancing the purpose of God is the issue of discipleship and possessions. Poverty and wealth stand out as critical concerns for the work of God, and Jesus addresses these subjects relentlessly in the Gospel of Luke.[9]

A poor man called Jesus?

Was Jesus himself economically disadvantaged? Sentimental pictures have been painted of his lowly beginnings in a stable, as though he were homeless, but these are based on misreadings of the Lukan narrative. Luke 2:1–7 portrays a small town

---

[9] Note: (1) the terminology of poverty congregates especially in Luke–Acts: πενιχρός – Luke 21:2 (otherwise absent in the New Testament); ἐνδεής – Acts 4:34 (otherwise absent from the New Testament); and πτωχός – Luke 4:18; 6:20; 7:22; 14:13, 21; 16:20, 22; 18:22; 19:18; 21:3 (Matthew – 5x, Mark – 5x, John – 4x, Paul – 4x, James – 4x, Revelation – 2x); (2) Jesus' vocation is directed to "the poor" (4:18–19; 7:22); (3) the Third Gospel shares with the other Synoptic Evangelists material on wealth and possessions (e.g., Mark 10:21, 25//Luke 18:22, 25; Mark 12:13–17//Luke 20:20–26; Mark 12:41//Luke 21:1–4; Matt. 5:40, 42//Luke 6:29–30; Matt. 6:25–33//Luke 12:22–32; Matt. 8:20//Luke 9:58); and (4) the Third Gospel contains a number of other, unique passages – e.g., Mary's Song (1:46–55); the first blessing with its corresponding woe (6:20, 24); further instruction on giving and receiving (6:27–36); the story of the rich fool (12:13–21); the parable of the shrewd manager and related material (16:1–13); the story of the rich man and Lazarus (16:19–26); the question of guests at dinner (14:13, 21); and the encounter between Jesus and Zacchaeus (19:1–10). For recent surveys, see François Bovon, *Luke the Theologian: Thirty-Three Years of Research (1950–1983)*, PTMS 12 (Allison Park, Pennsylvania: Pickwick, 1987) 390–400; John R. Donahue, "Two Decades of Research on the Rich and Poor in Luke–Acts," in *Justice and the Holy: Essays in Honor of Walter Harrelson*, ed. Douglas A. Knight and Peter J. Paris (Atlanta: Scholars, 1989) 129–44.

swelled by the requirements of the Rome-instigated census. As Bethlehem probably had no public inns, Luke envisages a near-eastern peasant home in which family and animals slept in one enclosed space, with the animals located on a lower level. Mary and Joseph, then, would have been the guests of family or friends, but their home would have been so over-crowded that, upon his birth, the baby was placed in a feeding trough.[10]

More to the point is the sacrifice offered by Jesus' parents in 2:24: "a pair of turtledoves or two young pigeons" – according to Lev. 12:8 the prescribed offering for those unable to afford a yearling lamb. Furthermore, in his Galilean ministry Jesus is said to depend on the support of others (8:1–3). Later, on the way to Jerusalem, Jesus says of himself that he has no place to lay his head (9:58), presumably an assertion about his lack of a home, but surely also a warning concerning the rejection to be expected of those who follow in his footsteps.

Jesus' dependence on the benefaction of others (8:3) has already ruled out any picture in Luke of an ascetic Jesus who rejects outright the use of wealth. To this may be added the refrain of his participation in dinner parties sufficiently ample that he could be characterized by others as a glutton and a drunkard (7:34; cf., e.g., 7:36; 11:37; 14:1–24; 19:1–27). In fact, throughout the Gospel Jesus interacts with peasants and with the wealthy; all are needful of God's good news.

Wealth and power

If wealth is not evil in and of itself, why does Jesus regard it as dangerous? What lies behind his warning that no one can serve both Mammon and God (16:13)? Why is it hard for those with wealth to enter the kingdom of God (18:24)? Why must would-be disciples give up everything (14:33)? Clearly for Luke, wealth presents itself as a temptation to prestige and security apart from God and for this reason is suspect (e.g.,

---

[10] See Joel B. Green, *The Gospel of Luke*, NICNT (Grand Rapids, Michigan: Wm. B. Eerdmans, forthcoming).

12:13–21, 33–34). Two aspects of ancient Mediterranean life help us to grapple more deeply with the problems Luke addresses.[11]

First, economic sharing was embedded in social relations. To share with someone without expectation of return was to treat them as though they were kin, family. Conversely, to refuse to share with others was tantamount to relating to them as though they were outside one's community. Hence, in 18:18–23, when the rich ruler refused to sell what he had and give the proceeds to the poor, he was making not only an economic decision but a social one as well. In essence, in choosing to preserve his own wealth he distanced himself from those in need – an action that is outside the bounds of discipleship in a Gospel where God has declared his salvific purpose to be realized in raising up the lowly and filling the hungry with good things (1:52–53). In making this decision, the ruler has opened up a wide chasm between himself and the regal prophet, Jesus, who has been sent to bring good news to the poor (4:18–19).

In such a context, "almsgiving" cannot be understood according to modern lexicons as "charity" or "missionary giving." Rather, giving to the poor was a signifier of social relations with the poor. For this reason, the Pharisees and scribes are soundly reprimanded for practices of non-sharing, practices that give way to acts of greed and wickedness (11:39–41; 20:46–47). For the same reason, the rich man, whose distance from the beggar Lazarus was maintained by the gate of his estate, finds himself after death in Hades (16:19–31).

Second, in insisting that giving takes place in a context where one retains no expectation of return, Jesus strikes at the root of one of the most prevalent models of friendship in antiquity, the patron–client relationship.[12] In this environment, a potential patron possessed some commodity required by a client. In exchange, the client would provide appropriate

---

[11] See above, ch. 1

[12] For this discussion, see Joel B. Green, "Caring as Gift and Goal: Biblical and Theological Reflections," in *The Crisis of Care: Affirming and Restoring Caring Practices in the Helping Professions*, ed. Susan S. Phillips, HCPE (Georgetown: Georgetown University, 1994) in press.

expressions of honor and loyalty to the patron. The point is that, having received patronage, the client now existed in a state of obligation, of debt. The possibilities for exploitation and the exercise of controlling, coercive power are high.

Jesus sets himself and his message over against this way of life, contrasting the behavior that characterizes everyday life in his world with behavior that grows out of service in the kingdom of God. The contrast is explicit in the structure of a central passage in the Sermon on the Plain (6:27–36). First, Jesus commands, "Love your enemies, do good to those who hate you," juxtaposing this statement with the question, "If you love those who love you, what credit is that to you?" Similarly, his charge, "Bless those who curse you, pray for those who abuse you. And if anyone strikes you on the cheek, offer the other one as well; likewise, if anyone takes your coat from you, do not hold back your shirt," is set over against his observation, "If you do good only to those who are good to you, what credit is that to you?" Finally, parallel to his assertion, "Give to everyone who begs from you," stands his final question, "If you lend to those from whom you hope to receive in return, what good is that to you?" In each case, those whose goodness grows out of the system of patronage – give to those who give to you, in order to build up a series of claims over others – are said to be no better than sinners. Jesus thus challenges his listeners not to act like outsiders, but like God's people. In doing so, he urges them to refuse the coercive, control-dominated system of relationships characteristic of the wider world.

This message is well summarized in the petition in Luke's version of the Lord's Prayer, "And forgive us our sins, for we ourselves forgive everyone indebted to us" (11:4). In this case, "debt" must be understood within the framework of patronal friendships. Consequently, Jesus is urging his followers to forgive debts – that is, to treat one another as kin, giving freely, not holding over one another obligations for praise and esteem.

It is not that Jesus denies how deeply ingrained in his world the patron–client system is. Instead, he *both* recognizes that people of his culture understand that this is the way the world works, *and* capitalizes on this way of thinking. Thus, having juxtaposed two ways of relating to people in the world, he goes on to suggest why his audience should adopt this new set of practices: "Your reward will be great, and you will be children of the Most High" (6:35). At this point, Jesus is actually working from within the model of benefaction. He says, in effect: give freely to one another, without holding over the head of your neighbors your claim on them; for God will take up their cause, and he will pay you what is due. In this economy, God is the Supreme Benefactor.

Similar instruction appears in ch. 14, where people are urged to invite outcasts to their luncheons and dinners; it is true, they will not receive repayment from those people, but God will repay them (14:12–14). The shrewd steward of 16:1–9 understands this way of thinking too. By placing people in his debt while serving as manager of their debts, he can guarantee their future hospitality (16:4). Similarly, Jesus observes, people can guarantee God's future, eternal hospitality by assisting the poor in the present (16:9).

This is not the end of the story, however. Jesus is trying to take the center of gravity for life away from the deeply rooted social systems of his day and to do so he is willing to use those systems while turning them on their head. At the same time, he is concerned to communicate a more fundamental motivation for gracious behavior: "God is kind to the ungrateful and the wicked. Be merciful, just as your Father is merciful" (6:35–36). In other words, be like God in your actions. God does not withhold goodness from those who reject him, from those who will not return his love. Neither should you. Let God's own character mold your character, your behavior.

Luke's material on the rich and poor, then, is woven into a larger fabric than talk of money and treasure might at first suggest. Wealth is intricately spun together with issues of status, power, and social privilege. For this reason it cannot remain long outside the purview of the gospel. Entry into the way of discipleship raises immediately the question of possessions, with Luke calling for an economic redistribution in which the needy are cared for and the wealthy give without expectation of return.[13]

EGALITARIAN COMMUNITY

Our discussion of faith and wealth has already been pushing the boundaries into a closely related question – namely, the shape of the community of disciples who together follow Jesus on the way. We have observed the degree to which this community cannot have closely prescribed boundaries. Jesus himself disallows any such concerns by his willingness to open the doors of discipleship to anyone, even (or especially) to those ordinarily excluded in the thinking of holy people. For Luke, this openness is to be embodied concretely at the table, as "the poor, the crippled, the blind, and the lame" together with those from "the roads and lanes" (14:21, 23) are welcomed. Indeed, it is precisely Jesus' radical openness in table fellowship in the Gospel of Luke that stands as a model and reproach to the Christian community in Acts as it struggles with crossing ethnic and religious lines at the table.

Status-seeking

One of the table scenes in Luke, prominent because of its timing just before Jesus' execution, involves Jesus eating with his disciples, then engaging them in extended table-talk (22:14–38). At the head of this discussion is the disciples' dispute over which among them is the greatest. This problem had surfaced in 9:46, but clearly remains a live issue even at the Last Supper.

Jesus adopts two different strategies to get at this problem. First, in 9:46–48, he employed a little child as an object-lesson, insisting, "Whoever welcomes this child in my name welcomes me, and whoever welcomes me welcomes the one who sent me; for the least among you all is the greatest." Given the status of

---

[13] Halvor Moxnes, *The Economy of the Kingdom: Social Conflict and Economic Relations in Luke's Gospel*, OBT (Philadelphia, Fortress, 1988).

children in Roman antiquity, this lesson must have come as a shock to the disciples. Simply put, children were "not adults." They might be valued for their present or future contribution to the family's livelihood, but were viewed as irrational, without emotional control, and as possessing little intrinsic value as human beings. This accounts for the widespread abandonment of children and for the practice of infanticide by which family size might be regulated in antiquity.[14] If "children" stands as a cipher for "those of lowest status," "welcoming," calls to mind the respect one gives to honored guests. In 7:44-46 welcoming is said to involve providing for the washing of feet, a kiss of greeting, oil to anoint the head. All of this for a child? In effect, Jesus asks his disciples to reorient their understanding of the way the world works by extending respectful service to the very group most often overlooked in society at large.

Second, in 22:24-27, he contrasts two kings and two kingdoms. On the one hand are the "kings of the Gentiles" who "lord it over" their subjects. They claim to be benefactors and so, according to the patron–client script, they practice coercive power and invite for themselves lavish praise. They give to their subjects, in other words, but they do so in exchange for still greater power and homage. On the other is Jesus himself. He recognizes that within the group of his disciples, he is the greater. Yet he presents himself as the one who serves, echoing the earlier picture of the returning master who serves his faithful slaves (12:37). In his kingdom, the link between status and service is disentangled. Even those who will sit on thrones of judgment (22:28-29) have, in this kingdom, no claim to status greater than any other. Both leaders and those who follow them are doing nothing more than what was assigned, with the result that neither may use their obedience as an occasion for demanding greater honor or elevated status (17:7-10).

It is for this reason that disciples are warned to beware of the

---

[14] See, e.g., Beryl Rawson, ed., *The Family in Ancient Rome: New Perspectives* (Ithaca, New York: Cornell University Press, 1986); Beryl Rawson, ed., *Marriage, Divorce, and Children in Ancient Rome* (Oxford University Press, 1991).

scribes (20:45–47). Scribes appear in public areas – market-place, synagogue, and banquet room – with the symbols of honor appropriate to their contexts, in order to invite defer-ence and respect (cf. 11:43; 14:7–11). But Jesus knows that the scribes are not distinctive in this regard, for all share in the tendency toward seeking recognition and public esteem. Even the disciples find themselves in a contest of honor, but such behavior only likens them to scribes. The community of dis-ciples must repudiate those underlying values and disassociate themselves from such practices. They follow a different way, the way of the Lord, the way of one who gave himself not in seeking honor but in giving it to the poor, the outcast, the marginalized, the lost, on account of his single-minded com-mitment to the redemptive purpose of God.

The new community and the Roman world

When Jesus set his kingdom over against "the kings of the Gentiles" (22:25) he was not only engaging in an interesting object-lesson. To a degree not often recognized, the values and behavior for which Jesus calls in Luke are contradictory to and even put in question the existence of the Roman Empire in his day.[15]

Luke's critique of Rome is fundamental. To see this it is necessary first to recognize that after the final victory of Octa-vian in the civil wars (27 BCE), Rome was unified not simply under one emperor but also by a political order based on the ethic of patronage. Octavian took for himself the name Augustus (cf. Luke 2:1) as well as a series of other titles. He was known as *princeps* – that is, *the* patron of the Roman people. He also received the title *pater patriae* – that is, father of the land of fathers, thus conceptualizing the empire as a household indebted to him as its head. Note, for example, the Myrian

---

[15] Richard J. Cassidy takes a different line from the one presented here in order to argue that Luke presents Jesus as a threat to the socio-political structures of his day (*Jesus, Politics, and Society: A Study of Luke's Gospel* [Maryknoll, New York: Orbis, 1978]). See also Cassidy, *Society and Politics in the Acts of the Apostles* (Maryknoll, New York: Orbis, 1987).

inscription: "Divine Augustus Caesar, son of a god, imperator of land and sea, the benefactor and savior of the whole world."[16]

Thus, Augustus assumed for himself the role of benefactor, patron, a role which during this period was pervasive throughout the empire. Slaves were indebted to their master, the *paterfamilias* (i.e., the patriarch of an extended family). Sons were under the rule of their fathers, awaiting the death of their fathers so that they might ascend to the status of patriarchs. Clients were bound to their patrons, and often had clients of their own. Patrons shared clients, and so on. The network of overlapping obligation spread throughout the empire, ultimately with everyone indebted to the emperor as benefactor – either as a result of his direct patronage throughout the empire, or indirectly through the levels and webs of obligation that may be traced back to him.

But even the emperor had client status of a sort, for the hierarchy of patronal relations extended beyond the sphere of humans so as to include the gods. The gods had shown favor to Rome, and especially to the *princeps*, the patron, the emperor. He was not himself divine, but he was the recipient of the gods' patronage and served as their special agent. Thus, the reciprocity of patronal relations obligated slaves to masters, sons to fathers, the elite to the emperor, and the emperor, together with all of Rome, to the gods.

In this way the political order, the binding ethic of patronage, was rooted in the divine. The ethic of obligation found its legitimation in the gods themselves. It was sacred. To deviate from the sacred order, then, was not simply to involve oneself in a social imbroglio, but was a violation of the sacred order.[17]

The message of Jesus in Luke violates the sacred political order of the Roman world. What is more, it does so on the basis of a clash of kings and kingdoms. Luke has consistently

---

[16] David C. Braund, *Augustus to Nero: A Sourcebook on Roman History. 31 BC – AD 68* (London: Crook Helm, 1985) §66.

[17] See James R. Hollingshead, "'For Freedom Christ Has Set Us Free': Time and Metaphor in the Political Thought of the Apostle Paul" (Unpublished Ph.D. diss., University of California at Berkeley, 1993) 140–60; cf. David L. Tiede, "The Kings of the Gentiles and the Leader Who Serves: Luke 22:24–30," *WW* 12 (1992) 23–8.

presented Jesus as Son of God, God's own agent, whose life and message embodies God's own purpose. In calling into question the Roman social order, implicated as it was in the ethic of patronage, Jesus called into question the gods in whom that system received sanction *and* substituted in their stead the God of Abraham, the Lord of Israel, Yahweh.

The new community being established by Jesus is thus counter-cultural in the deepest sense. Their practices as a community, if they are to follow Jesus, would deviate radically from the Roman ethic and disavow its divine origin. Importantly, this denunciation of Rome is not characterized by violence, according to Luke's theology. To take up arms, to exert coercive force, would be to adopt a style of life consistent with the Roman way, not with the way of this new kingdom breaking into the world. Indeed, one of Jesus' severest criticisms of the scribes and Pharisees is that they act too much like Romans in their claims to honor and desire for status as benefactors. Toward the enemy, Jesus practices and counsels forgiveness, service, love, and care (cf. 6:27–36; 23:34). Service was the way of the Lord among his disciples (22:27). Service will be the way of the Lord in the future, at his return (12:37). And service is the way of the Lord for his followers now, in the interim.

The importance of Jesus' critique of the Roman social order with its divine moorings, in 22:24–27, is elevated when we locate this discussion more fully in its narrative setting. Immediately preceding the material in question is (1) the example of Peter and John who are delegated by Jesus to serve the band of disciples by preparing for them all a guest room in which to eat the Passover (22:7–13), and (2) the example of Jesus, whose service extends to the giving of his life in order to establish the new covenant (22:14–23). Following on from Jesus' instructions on status and servitude is his act of conferring on the disciples a kingdom (22:28–30) and the instruction to Simon about strengthening the disciples following their failure (22:31–34). These are images of leadership, and Jesus' message is designed to qualify the character of that leadership: not like the Gentiles, but like Jesus. Not their kingdoms but the kingdom of God. Not status-minded benefaction, but giving freely, without any concern for repayment in honor or status.

CHAPTER 6

"That you may know the truth":
Luke's Gospel in the church

The influence of the Gospel of Luke in Western society is already striking. Musicians and artists of every era have returned to Luke's narrative of the nativity for images of divine–human encounter. Even in the rapidly emerging post-Christian society of the late twentieth century, people of all ages may still know something of the story that begins, "In the days of Caesar Augustus ..." (Luke 2:1). Many of the best-loved and most widely known stories of Jesus appear in the Third Gospel, but are absent in the Gospels of Matthew, Mark, and John. The Story of the Prodigal Son, the Story of the Good Samaritan, the Emmaus Road episode, Jesus' prayer from the cross, "Father, forgive them ..." (23:34) – these are a few of the peculiarly Lukan stories of Jesus known to and influential for both the Christian church and the wider public.

It must be acknowledged, though, that such examples as these point much more to the influence of Lukan material than to the influence of the Gospel of Luke as such. That is, these stories seem to have circulated in the church and world in, as it were, disembodied form, divorced from their narrative place-ment in the Third Gospel. This is a consequence, at least partially, of the atomistic way the Gospel has been read – or perhaps better, "mined" for nuggets of inspiration and truth. Not often in the history of Gospels' study has the Gospel of Luke been read "from left to right," "from start to finish," as a narrative whole. Already in the second century it was being employed as a repository from which one might draw infor-mation about Jesus. Otherwise, Calvin's treatment illustrates the fate of the Gospel for centuries; his massive commentary on the Bible allotted one volume to the Gospels of Matthew, Mark, and Luke, read together as the story of Jesus. In his *Explanatory Notes upon the New Testament* (1754), John Wesley understood Luke to give "the history of Christ, from His coming into the world to His ascension into heaven."[1]

This interpretive history is not altogether problematic, of course. The quest of the historical Jesus is significant to a faith such as ours, grounded as it is in the historical encounter between God and humanity, God and the material world, in Jesus of Nazareth.[2] And it is especially though not quite exclusively via the canonical Gospels that we have access to traditions of Jesus' life.[3] Hence, if we are to take up the fundamental challenge of the Gospel – namely, to communicate the relevance of Jesus to new audiences – we must return again and again to these stories, both to grapple with the data available to us through them but also to see in what ways these Evangelists have already paved the way, by shaping the story of Jesus for communication in new settings.

In saying this, however, we have already hinted at why an atomistic reading of the Gospel of Luke can be troublesome. The Third Gospel is a "partial" account – partial both in the sense of being incomplete and in the sense of being committed to a perspective.[4] The Third Evangelist has included this material, excluded other; "ordered" his account in this way, not in that. This is not a neutral, disinterested chronicle but a partisan narrative shaping of the story of Jesus. His aim is communicative in the sense of his purpose to engage his audience in discourse and so to shape them by his work.

[1] John Wesley, *Explanatory Notes upon the New Testament* (London: Epworth, 1976 [1754]) 196. John Drury sketches a history of the interpretation of the Third Gospel, focusing especially on the period from the advent of source criticism (19th century) to the ascent of redaction criticism (1950s–1980s), in "Luke, Gospel of," in *A Dictionary of Biblical Interpretation*, ed. R. J. Coggins and J. L. Houlden (London: SCM; Philadelphia: Trinity, 1990) 410–14.

[2] Cf. I. Howard Marshall, *I Believe in the Historical Jesus* (London: Hodder and Stoughton; Grand Rapids, Michigan: Wm. B. Eerdmans, 1977).

[3] Cf., e.g., David Wenham, ed., *The Jesus Tradition outside the Gospels*, GP 5 (Sheffield: JSOT, 1984).

[4] For this distinction, see James Clifford, "Introduction: Partial Truths," in *Writing Culture: The Poetics and Politics of Ethnography*, ed. James Clifford and George E. Marcus (Berkeley/Los Angeles/London: University of California, 1986) 1–26.

As discourse the Gospel of Luke aims to have particular effects as a Gospel on its audience. Hence, for example, the Story of the Prodigal Son (15:11–32) may speak to us while dislocated from its narrative co-text, but when heard within the framework of the Gospel of Luke, and especially within its local co-text, 15:1–32, it may be heard differently. Today, a number of people struggle with the Story of the Prodigal Son because of their own family histories; set within the narrative framework of Luke 15, though, the question of "belonging" takes on much greater significance, imploring us to examine in what ways we might be refusing to celebrate the welcoming of the apparently unfaithful into the family. Set within its narrative framework, the Story of the Prodigal Son may grip us in new and transformative ways. Similarly, as we have seen, when heard within the larger framework of Luke 1–2, "in the days of Caesar Augustus . . ." (2:1) is a phrase that sounds suddenly less affable, less disarming; it acquires a menacing tone, reminding us of Luke's depiction of God's people in enemy hands, longing for deliverance.

LUKE AND THE NEW TESTAMENT

One way of addressing the question of the larger significance of the theology of the Gospel of Luke is to listen for the similarities and distinctiveness of Luke's voice within the choir of other New Testament voices. Although the various New Testament writers bear witness to the same gospel, they do so while addressing their own socio-historical exigencies and from within already diverse ecclesiastical communities. In what areas might Luke's witness be compared profitably with that of other New Testament writers?

One of the areas to which New Testament students have often drawn attention with respect to Luke's distinctiveness is soteriology – that is, his understanding of salvation and, especially, of his understanding of the relationship of the crucifixion of Jesus to redemption. The Second Evangelist presents as a climactic point of his Gospel the well-known "ransom saying": "For the Son of Man came not to be served, but to serve, and to give his life as a ransom for many" (Mark 10:45). Even if this saying comes at the close of a Markan section on Jesus' teaching on servitude, it nonetheless underscores the significance of Jesus' death as redemptive. Similarly, Paul situates the redemptive consequence of the cross of Christ at the center of his understanding of Jesus and salvation. "Christ died for (us) (our sins)" is a cardinal affirmation in Pauline thought (cf., e.g., Rom. 5:6, 8; 14:9; 1 Cor. 8:11; 15:3; 2 Cor. 5:14–15; Gal. 2:21; 1 Thess. 5:10).

Luke, however, has not incorporated the ransom saying into his Gospel, a reality that grows in importance if in fact Luke made use of the Gospel of Mark in writing his own narrative. The closest substitute appears in Luke 19:10: "The Son of Man came to seek and to save the lost." *How* the Son of Man "saves the lost" is not clarified in this saying. In fact, even though the pivotal character of Jesus' execution in redemptive history is emphatic for Luke, how it functions has not been so clear.

One must turn to Acts to learn anything more conclusive concerning the basis for the offer of salvation in Lukan thought. There it becomes evident that Jesus' exaltation (i.e., his resurrection, but perhaps also his ascension) is for Luke the preeminent salvific event (e.g., Acts 2:33; 5:30–31).

In a comparison of Lukan theology with other New Testament voices, two points are of interest here. First, the Lukan narrative is not completely divested of interest in the atoning work of Jesus (cf. Luke 22:19–20; Acts 20:28), but the weight of interest falls solidly on Jesus' resurrection. Second, although for Paul the cross of Christ is central, Jesus' crucifixion does appear in Paul in tandem with his resurrection. And, as such, the resurrection, too, can be accorded redemptive significance (e.g., Rom. 4:24–25; 2 Cor. 5:15; cf. 1 Thess. 1:9–10). Hence, although Luke's emphasis is evident, it is equally clear that his is not a lone voice on this matter.

Second, like almost every other New Testament book, the Gospel of Luke too is occupied with "the Gentile problem." The possibility and/or conditions of God's full acceptance of persons from all nations, whether Jew or Gentile, was clearly a matter of intense debate in apostolic Christianity (cf., e.g., Acts

15; Galatians). In resolving this issue, in favor of full acceptance without the need for conversion first to Judaism, the voice
of Paul was of major, perhaps decisive, significance. Paul saw
his own divine vocation as intimately related to the Gentile
mission (e.g., Gal. 2:8), the collection for the saints in Jerusalem as a concrete expression of the unity of Jew and Gentile
in the gospel (e.g., Rom. 15:25–32; 2 Cor. 8–9), and, indeed,
the mission to the Gentiles as a natural outworking of God's
covenant with Abraham and of the righteousness of God (esp.
Galatians and Romans).

In his second volume, Acts, Luke dealt with the question of
the Gentiles more straightforwardly. In the Third Gospel, one
finds only rare references to Gentile persons, though these can
be quite positive in their appreciation of Gentile faith and/or
perception (e.g., 7:1–10; 23:47). The infrequency with which
Gentiles are mentioned is no measure of their lack of importance even at this stage of the Lukan enterprise, however.
Although Jesus does not much interact with Gentiles in Luke,
the path for full acceptance of Gentiles is well laid by the
Gospel's depiction of the ministry of Jesus. In the Third
Gospel, "Gentiles" may be understood as members of a more
encompassing category of persons generally understood to be
outside the boundaries of divine graciousness. This list would
include lepers, Samaritans, the sick, women, "sinners," toll-
collectors, children, Gentiles, and others – that is, persons
normally excluded from the religious circles of the pious but, in
Luke's depiction, welcome in the community of Jesus' followers. That is, in the Third Gospel, Luke's treatment of "the
problem of the Gentiles" is foremost a subset of his more
general concern with the universalism of grace proffered
through Jesus' mission.

A further matter of importance in a comparison of Luke's
theology with other New Testament theologies is in the area of
eschatology. As we have seen, on this theme Lukan theology is
very much at home within the framework of New Testament
eschatology as a whole, even if Luke's perspective is nuanced in
its own way. Paul locates the lives of believers on a continuum
between the "no longer" and the "not yet," between the

death/resurrection of Jesus and his parousia. For Paul, then, present life is grounded in the salvific activity of Jesus, and is a foretaste and promise of the fullness of life with God. Luke can also think in terms of future consummation (12:32–56; 17:20–37; 21:5–36). On the continuum of emphasis between the present experience of salvation and its future culmination, however, Luke is oriented more toward the present. His thought is thus more akin to that of the Fourth Gospel than to that of Paul.

Luke is not as clear as Paul (or the other Synoptic Evangelists) that Jesus' return is soon. His emphasis, instead, is on the certainty but unpredictability of the consummation of the kingdom and so on the need always to be faithful. No doubt this is related to his understanding of the gospel that situates the experience of salvation above all in the present. In Johannine language, "eternal life" extends into the present (cf. John 3:16; 10:10). In Lukan language, "Salvation has come to this house *today*" (19:9; cf., e.g., 4:21; 23:43). For the Third Evangelist, if the acceptance and empowerment of salvation are already at work, so also is the responsibility to faithful service and mission already present. Eschatology is enlisted in the service of discipleship.

Finally, we may draw attention to the life of discipleship. In Lukan terms, what are "the fruits of repentance" by which children of Abraham, followers of Jesus, are known? We have already devoted a chapter to discipleship in the Gospel of Luke, so it is only necessary at this point to emphasize one or two Lukan distinctives.

First, of course, is the Lukan emphasis on faith and wealth. In the New Testament, not only does the vocabulary of wealth and poverty especially congregate in the Third Gospel, not only does Luke record material otherwise unknown to us regarding Jesus' teaching on faith and wealth, but the very mission of Jesus is characterized as "bringing good news to the poor" (4:18). The Epistle of James has a similar emphasis on the importance of faithful responses *vis-à-vis* the poor, and the Book of Revelation contains a pronounced and ongoing critique of wealth (e.g., Rev. 3:17–18; 18). Paul, too, deals with issues of wealth and faith, though most often he does so either in relation to the collection for Jerusalem (Gal. 2:9–10; 1 Cor. 16:1–4; 2 Cor. 7:14–9:15; Rom. 15:25–32) or indirectly with reference to patronal relations (a key issue in the Corinthian correspondence and, quite differently, in Philippians).[5] But the treatment of faith and wealth in the Third Gospel is at once more pervasive and more complex.

Luke offers no straightforward answer to the problem of possessions and the life of faith, but instead invites the community of believers into reflection on the place of the poor among them. He also encourages reflection on how repentance and faith might work themselves out concretely with respect to "everything that one has." If there is a bottom line for Luke, it is that nothing – no possession, no relationship, no commitment, nothing – can take the place of one's relationship to Jesus and the in-breaking kingdom of God as that which determines day-to-day behavior. As an immediate and necessary corollary, Luke highlights the ever-present challenge and need to place "everything one has" in the service of God's purpose, especially by befriending those living in need. This is not far from James' notion of showing that one has faith by one's practices with respect to the poor (e.g., James 2).

Luke also emphasizes the life of discipleship as a life open to the work of God in and through others, especially those often defined as living outside the gracious activity of God. In comparison with other New Testament writers, Luke gives a particularly important place to women as disciples and so as persons who have an important contribution to make to the community of Jesus' followers. Women are conspicuous in the Gospel of Luke, and they appear more often than not as exemplars of faith and faithfulness, sometimes in contrast to male disciples (e.g., 24:1–11). Although women have such an important role to play in Luke it is also true, as in Paul, that the range of possibilities open to women in the Third Gospel is limited. In Paul and the larger Pauline circle, limitations are

---

[5] See Peter Marshall, *Enmity in Corinth: Social Conventions in Paul's Relations with the Corinthians*, WUNT 2.33 (Tübingen: J. C. B. Mohr [Paul Siebeck], 1987).

presented by way of negative commands (e.g., 1 Cor. 14:33–36; cf. 1 Tim. 2:9–15). No such boundaries are dictated in the Gospel of Luke; rather, limitations to the place of women are presented indirectly, via the absence of women in public leadership and/or as public spokespersons of the faith (cf. John 4:4–30). In this, we see the degree to which both Luke and Paul are participants in the first-century Greco-Roman world.

HEARING THE GOSPEL OF LUKE TODAY

How can the Gospel of Luke be heard as God's Word today? That is, how might we appropriate this narrative, especially as a theological document? First, we must realize that, quite apart from the benefit of hermeneutical reflection, Lukan material is already being heard today. It is already serving as a transformative text in our world. The theological movement popularized in the latter half of the twentieth century – first ascertain what it meant in its first-century context, then explore what it means in this new context[6] – is self-evidently artificial in the practice of reading biblical texts. This is especially true for biblical interpretation within communities of faith, who see in "this story" *their* story, visualizing themselves as nothing more or less than the continuation of *those* communities of faith. In the biblical texts, these communities see how Christian identity is construed via narratives that are historically grounded in another time and place, but continue to exhibit redemptive power in the present.[7]

Even more broadly, though, the influence of, say, the story of the Good Samaritan (10:30–35) in wider (at least American) society is utterly profound. As Robert Wuthnow has learned, this parable has become "one of those ancient myths that embodies the deepest meanings in our culture. In learning it and reshaping it we define what it means to be com-

---

[6] Cf. Krister Stendahl, "Biblical Theology, Contemporary," in *IDB* 1:418–32.
[7] For the notion of continuity of the Christian community from its beginnings to the present and the eschaton as a hermeneutical motto, see James Wm. McClendon Jr., *Systematic Theology*, vol. 1: *Ethics* (Nashville: Abingdon, 1986) 31–35.

passionate."[8] From his social-scientific analysis of American altruism and caring activity, he discovered a positive relationship between charitable behavior and familiarity with the story of the Good Samaritan. Even people who profess no connection with the church whatsoever, even people who cannot recite the story in recognizable form, nevertheless continue to speak of "the Good Samaritan effect." It may be argued that boiling this parable down to "a character who showed compassion" misses the arresting point of the story, especially when this parable is read in its Lukan co-text. But this does not detract from the reality that this segment of the Third Gospel has already found its way into public discourse at a taken-for-granted level.

Second, it is nevertheless of importance that we inquire into the possibility of a more reflective, critical appropriation of the Lukan message. This involves our respecting the Lukan enterprise so as to accept its invitation to enter into the world of Luke, to adopt a perspective from within the narrative. In this way, we leave ourselves open to the possibility of hearing Luke so as to participate in its vision of partnership in the service of God's purpose. To enter Luke's narrative world in this way, of course, is to de-center our own self-interests so as to be addressed by the text as "other," to allow it to engage us in creative discourse, to take the risk of being shaped, indeed transformed in the encounter.[9]

This does not mean that we lose ourselves in the Lukan narrative, however. The Gospel of Luke is a first-century document from the Mediterranean world; we are twentieth-century people, many of us from quite different worlds. Understanding how the message of Luke articulates with and challenges its world may shed light on our own experience of the world and of God. Sometimes this will happen directly. For example, in the words of the wealthy agriculturalist of Luke 12:16–19 – "What should I do, for I have no place to store my

---

[8] Robert Wuthnow, *Acts of Compassion: Caring for Others and Helping Ourselves* (Princeton University Press, 1991) 161; see ch. 6.

[9] Cf. Anthony C. Thiselton, *New Horizons in Hermeneutics* (London: Collins; Grand Rapids, Michigan: Zondervan, 1992) 16–29.

crops?" – we may hear the exercise of decision-making in an individualistic way, apart from the larger community; separated from his community by his wealth, this landowner lives under the illusion that he is self-sufficient, not requiring even divine help. If we can hear such nuances, we may also find reason to question our own individualistic proclivities. In other cases, the analogy of situation may be less straightforward. We come as late-twentieth-century people with our own needs and questions, not assuming that Luke's questions are ours, but inquiring into the strategies, sources of authority, and contours of Luke's presentation that might inform our own communities of faithful discourse.

Third, our attempts at appropriating the message of Luke will be richer if we are able to attend to the promise of "a storied theology," but also if we take seriously the varieties of literary forms resident within Luke's larger narrative. This means, on the one hand, that we must resist attempts to alleviate the tension that often appears in Luke's discourse. Who is responsible for Jesus' death? It is ordained by God (e.g., 9:22; 22:22), required by the Jewish leaders (22:1–5, 52; 22:66–23:5, 10), carried out by the Roman military (23:25, 33, 36; Acts 2:23), set in motion by Judas (22:6, 47–48), a disclosure of diabolic power (22:3, 28, 40, 46, 53; 23:44), and accepted by Jesus (22:42). "Story," like few other literary forms, is able to hold together such disparate forces without collapsing into one corner the complex network of forces and motivations informing the human–divine relationship. It is hard to reduce "story" to a formula. A sensitive reading of Luke's message will show awareness of this ambiguity and represent the same in reflective appropriation of Luke's theology.

At the same time, within this narrative presentation one finds a variety of literary forms or genres that not only must be read in genre-appropriate ways, but might also be appropriated along different lines. For example, the temptation always is to boil "parable" down to its one, true meaning, neglecting the built-in polysemy of parable that allows it to speak at multiple levels and along multiple paths. In some cases, Jesus' message was so hard-hitting, so confrontational, that almost of necessity it had to be wrapped in the layered skins of parable. Teased by parable into ongoing reflection, his audience could be invited into an interpretive dance leading them from the comfort of the status quo to self-criticism to personal and social transformation. As we learn to hear Luke, perhaps we can be shaped too, so as to refuse the temptation of dispensing easy answers in favor of inviting people to reflect together in community on the depth and pertinence of this message. To pursue this example, perhaps the best way to appropriate critically the message of parable is to tell a parable.

Fourth, and to make more explicit an earlier point, we engage in a reflective appropriation of the Lukan message not simply (and sometimes not at all) by reading the content of his message into our world, but also (and sometimes only) by inquiring into how Luke himself has engaged in the task of theology and ethics. This is true above all because Luke is concerned to shape a community that discerns, embraces, and serves the divine purpose more than he is to outline in detail the precise beliefs and habits of that community. In writing the Gospel, Luke bears witness to the divine visitation that makes redemption and redemptive community possible, and invites persons to participate as co-workers in this redemptive aim – not to render his audience dependent on him as a kind of "teacher of righteousness." Perhaps more intuitively this is true because Luke addresses some issues that are of little direct significance in our worlds (where, for example, Emperor Augustus and the Jerusalem temple are no more), but he does not address other issues that have become pressing in some of our communities (the ordination of homosexuals and the ramifications of the Human Genome Project, for example).

In his study *Communities of Discourse*, Robert Wuthnow has drawn attention to a helpful approach to questions of this sort. Although he is concerned with the Protestant Reformation, the Enlightenment, and the rise of European socialism, his methodological considerations are equally appropriate to a reading of Luke's narrative.[10] He characterizes his investigation as a study of the problem of articulation – that is, how ideas can both be shaped by their social situations and yet manage to disengage from and often challenge those very situations. In the case of the aspirations of Luke we might ask, how can the Third Gospel be situated in and reflect a particular socio-historical environment while at the same time working to undermine that environment? How can Luke gain for his narrative a hearing among a people whose understanding of "the way the world works" is being subverted by that narrative? What strategies does he adopt? How has he engaged in theological and ethical reflection? How has he invited his audience into the reflective and constructive task of discourse on discipleship? To what authorities does he appeal? What vision of "the new world" does he present; and how does he solicit contemplation on and service in that world? In short, to learn "Lukan theology" is to grapple with more than the content of the Lukan message; it is also to explore how Luke engages in the theological task and the strategies by which he engages his audience in transformative discourse.

Fifth, persons concerned today to appropriate the message of Luke will want to take seriously the presence of Luke in the four-fold Gospel canon. The New Testament includes not one "life of Jesus" but four narrative expressions of the one "gospel," Jesus Christ. One important corollary of this reality is that attempts to articulate the story of Jesus in audience-appropriate forms and language is sanctioned already by the form of the New Testament. In order to hear and communicate the gospel today, we must become "evangelical" in the sense of immersing ourselves in these accounts and by learning from them how to convey this gospel in our own world. What shape would "gospel" take today? To take seriously Luke's canonical placement is also to accept its challenge to continue the

---

[10] Robert Wuthnow, *Communities of Discourse: Ideology and Social Structure in the Reformation, the Enlightenment, and European Socialism* (Cambridge, Massachusetts; London: Harvard University Press, 1989).

business of drawing people into a living encounter with Jesus of
Nazareth.[11]

Having arranged a number of coordinates for the task of
reflective appropriation of the message of Luke, we may
proceed now to outline a few elements of the Lukan message of
particular relevance in many Christian communities today.

SALVATION

Traditional understandings of Christian faith in the northern
hemisphere have generated a series of fissures – between the
horizontal and vertical, the spiritual and the secular, social
witness and evangelism, the personal and the public, individual sin and systemic sin, and the like. These have made
problematic our understanding of "salvation" and, thus,
"evangelism." Saved *from* what? Saved *to* what? Traditional
styles of evangelism concomitant with rifts of this nature have
emphasized proclamation to individuals and the initiation of
individuals into the heavenly reign of God.[12] "Salvation" in
this Christian subculture has generally been defined along
narrow lines, in subjective, individualistic terms.

Analogously, "good news to the poor" in wider society is
often understood as a matter of economic intervention, as
though the answer for "the poor" would be to transform them
into members of "the middle class." The needs of "the poor"
around issues of dignity and kinship are rarely entertained;
after all, did the psychologist Abraham Maslow not teach us
that there can be no "self-actualization" (itself often defined
outside of relational lines) without material security? The
problems represented by hunger and homelessness in the West
are frequently dissected along biographical lines: how did this
person find herself living on the street? What irresponsible
decisions did he make that left him without a roof for his

---

[11] Joel B. Green, *How to Read the Gospels and Acts* (Downers Grove, Illinois: Inter-
Varsity, 1987) 25–29.

[12] Cf. Priscilla Pope-Levison, *Evangelization from a Liberation Perspective*, AUS 7, TR 69
(New York/Bern/Frankfurt-on-Main: Peter Lang, 1991); Pope-Levison, "Evangelism and Liberation: Perspectives from Latin America," *Catalyst* 15 (4, 1989) 3, 5.

family? Rendering the problem along individualistic lines, we also entertain a narrow band of solutions, themselves focused on individuals. The potential harm or help of cultural institutions – for example, the political economy, the public church, the almost hypostatized power of technology – rarely comes under scrutiny.

No doubt, our limited notions of salvation have been fed by the loosening and in many cases the breakdown of kinship and village ties ushered in with the onset of modernity. Framing the evangelistic task as "winning souls" and articulating salvation as a preeminently spiritual activity, in Protestant circles especially as the justification by faith of individuals, is naturally related in a cause–effect alliance to the modernist impulses of liberation-by-individuation and freedom through mobility and separation from social obligation.[13] Interestingly, such impulses have begun to come full circle. In many regions the ensuing isolation and alienation, felt and real, have become a problem to be addressed by the gospel, so that the psychological ramifications of the good news are more and more explored.[14] More and more, people of the West are learning the wisdom of the African proverb, "We are, therefore I am."[15]

A close reading of the Gospel of Luke indicates the degree to which the above-noted fractures in the message and aim of salvation are troublesome. Luke situates human salvation, even when understood in personal terms, within larger social conventions and institutions – a strategy foreign to many of us. An almost obligatory antagonism exists between our love affair with individualism and any suitable accounting for the role of institutions in our lives. "We think in the first place that the problem is probably with the individual; if not, then with the organization. This pattern of thinking hides from us the power of institutions and their great possibilities for good and for

---

[13] See the perceptive analysis of Robert N. Bellah *et al.*, *Habits of the Heart: Individualism and Commitment in American Life* (Berkeley: University of California Press, 1985).

[14] For one suggestive program for integrating psychology and the gospel of Jesus Christ, see Margaret G. Alter, *Resurrection Psychology* (Chicago: Loyola University Press, 1994).

[15] Cited in Anton Wessels, *Images of Jesus: How Jesus Is Perceived and Portrayed in Non-European Cultures* (Grand Rapids, Michigan: Wm. B. Eerdmans, 1990) 96.

evil."[16] This pattern of thinking also keeps us from reflecting fully on how the divine intervention of God in the world might condemn and/or redeem our institutions. (By "institutions" we mean both patterns of expected behavior reinforced by social sanctions and those organizational situations in which such behavior and the discourse surrounding it find embodiment and propagation.)[17] It is of great consequence that, when Luke presents his vision of salvation, he does so in language that embraces the eminent institutions of the larger Roman world of the first century.

As we have seen, divine deliverance, as Luke perceives it, overcomes diabolic forces that manifest themselves in human affairs in disease and brokenness that work against God's purpose. It reaches the acme of the empire itself, its patronal ethic and resulting polity, together with its divine legitimation in the gods. It sheds light on such dark places in Luke's world as the temple, whose architecture and powerful presence legitimates attitudes and behavior by which children, women, the sick, foreigners, and all who can be labeled as "others" by the holders and purveyors of power and privilege are held at arm's length from the gracious embrace of God. It subverts such pivotal cultural values as honor and shame and the general concern with status that drives a wedge between the would-be faithful and a demeanor that embodies that of the merciful Father. And it opens the way of personal renewal for the call to a form of discipleship realized within the community of discipleship oriented to service in and throughout the world. In the Lukan conception, life must be viewed in its totality, salvation understood in the most all-encompassing way possible. Luke holds together what the contemporary church has often partitioned into discordant elements: empowering the disadvantaged, seeking the lost, reconciling persons across social lines, calling people to repentance, healing the sick, forgiving sins, initiating people into the community of God's people. All of these and more are constitutive of salvation in the Third Gospel.

[16] Robert N. Bellah *et al.*, *The Good Society* (New York: Alfred A. Knopf, 1991) 11.
[17] Cf. Wuthnow, *Communities of Discourse*, 5–17; Bellah *et al.*, *Good Society*, 10–11.

US AND THEM

The Gospel of Luke opens with subtle reminders of the boundaries separating "us" and "them" – boundaries deeply rooted in the politico-economic world of the Mediterranean and in the ancient life of Israel (1:5, 8–9). There is, first, King Herod, wealthy landowner, representative of Rome, insulated from the larger world of Palestine by urban values and lifestyle. Second, there is Zechariah – a male Israelite born to the family of Aaron, his separation from other Israelites subtly represented by his selection not only to serve in the temple (his birthright as priest) but to enter the sanctuary of the Lord and offer incense (a great honor for a priest, one who is already a member of the honored caste of Israelites). This is only the beginning of the emphasis within Luke's world on the circles of inclusion and exclusion: priests and non-priests, legal experts and lay, powerful and weak, Jews and Samaritans, adults and children, clean and unclean, well and ill, and so on.

These examples depict the extraordinary importance placed in Luke's world on "belonging," on kinship and the notion of extended family (or fictive kinship). Those who belong share in the family's resources. A widow, on the other hand, is by definition without family, without resources, and is perilously vulnerable (cf. 7:11–17; 21:1–4).

The Gospel of Luke, as we have seen, highlights this concern with distinguishing between "us" and "them" in part to undercut it.

"Master," John answered, "we saw someone exorcising demons in your name, and we tried to stop him, for he is not a follower with us." He answered, "Do not stop him; for whoever is not against you is for you." (9:49–50)

Nevertheless, contemporary followers of Jesus may be astonished by this business of boundary-making. Believers, especially in mainline churches, and with them many persons in society as a whole accord privilege to openness, acceptance, pluralism. Does Luke's theological emphasis on the expansiveness of God's grace – e.g., on open table fellowship – simply affirm the increasingly open and pluralistic profile of our world?

Of course, one may point immediately to the seemingly omnipresent vestiges of racism across our world today – vestiges which seem to have taken on a reproductive life of their own, breeding racism in new forms and in new places. And to this may be added any number of other "-isms" – ageism, sexism, classism, and the like – by which our lives are compartmentalized from the lives of others within and outside the Christian community. Yet our increasing awareness of these forms of division is itself a manifestation of our increasingly pluralistic tendencies. At least, it may be argued, we are more conscious of the implicit assumptions behind some of our language and practices.

There is a more fundamental point: we must recognize how shallow our "pluralism" is. Although the dominant culture in a given region may have opened its arms to allow for the existence and proliferation of other groups, and perhaps even for social and ecclesial exchange with them, has this not proceeded on terms predetermined by the dominant group? And have not those terms borne within them, however implicitly, the necessary elements to ensure the ongoing superiority of the dominant?[18] If it is true that others have been invited to the table of discourse, is it not also true that it is precisely to the table of the dominant culture that they have been invited, where too "they" must use "our" vocabulary and stick with "our" topics of conversation? In spite of the rise of pluralism as a primary cultural virtue, boundary-making continues in multitudinous forms – whether one is thinking of communities structured along clannish lines on the west coast of the United States and the northeast coast of Scotland, of Western churches struggling with the genesis of truly indigenous faith communities of Jesus' disciples in the Pacific Islands, or of the determination of "outsiders" by any number of categories of language-usage or behavioral practices.

---

[18] See the perspicacious analysis of Pierre Bourdieu, *Language and Symbolic Power* (Cambridge, Massachusetts: Harvard University Press, 1991).

This is precisely the point at which American readings of the Good Samaritan story (see above) are most distressing. Failing to read the story against its own cultural horizon or within its co-text in the Third Gospel, the Good Samaritan becomes the prototype of "the compassionate person." This reading should not be underplayed in a world where physical security is increasingly less taken for granted, but it hardly grapples with the scandal of Luke's message. After all (to paraphrase), "If you show compassion to those of your own clique, what credit is that to you?" (6:27–34). Nor is Jesus' point simply that one should show compassion indiscriminately. Rather, he insists, "Love your enemies" (6:35). It is this injunction that he goes on to illustrate in the Story of the Good Samaritan, a story not of compassion from a friend but from an outsider, an enemy, one of "them." In this way, and in this co-text, Jesus' admonition, "Do not judge, and you will not be judged" (6:37) also makes sense. To paraphrase, "Do not let your predeterminations of friendship and family relationship circumscribe the good that you will show others." The point is not that we will not generate boundaries, but that we cannot expect that God will honor them; the person in need, whether enemy or family, whether "them" or "us," is present as an opportunity for the extension of God's boundless grace.

In fact, Luke's message throws into serious question contemporary practices of boundary-making *and* modern notions of "pluralism." Regarding the former, in the segregation of our lives from others not like us, we are not so far from the people of Luke's world as we might wish. Regarding the latter, it is imperative that we recognize Luke's interest in shaping a community whose "face is set" on serving God's aim. This theological interest of Luke's *is* boundary-making, for not all will choose so to order their lives. A "pluralism" that refuses to recognize the generation of such boundaries finds no support in Luke's Gospel. But the end of such boundary-making is not the proposed exclusion of persons from divine influence. God is kind to the ungrateful and the wicked too, and Jesus' disciples are to be distinguished by such scandalous grace (6:35–36).

THE PROBLEM OF ARTICULATION

In a prophetic book on the rise of the women's movement in the last four decades of the twentieth century, Suzanne Gordon decries what the movement has become.[19] Women, vitally concerned not merely with their own advancement but with the shaping of the world by inhumane values, entered the marketplace and corporate world with visions of serving as transformative agents. Competition, individual success, economic bottom-line thinking, and the like were to be tempered with care and compassion, the common good, concern for quality of life. She argues, though, that the women's movement has had little success in shaping the larger world, that the marketplace and corporate world have shaped women more than been shaped by them, and that women have too often betrayed their own values and commitments in order to fit in. "We have entered the male kingdom," she writes, "and yet, we have been forced to play by the king's rules"[20] – with the consequence that competition is privileged over caring, work above love, power above empowerment, personal wealth over human worth.

Gordon's analysis of the women's movement is parabolic of the church. As members of a minority movement, followers of Jesus have the opportunity to bring to the table of public discourse an alternative vision for life together. Given that such a vision will in large part be determined by the socio-historical exigencies of a Christian community, it may nonetheless disengage from those exigencies sufficiently to present values and sponsor practices that are counter-cultural. In the broader environment the danger of simple coalescence is omnipresent.

In the words of Robert Wuthnow, this is the "problem of articulation":

if cultural products do not articulate closely enough with their social settings, they are likely to be regarded by the potential audiences of which these settings are composed as irrelevant, unrealistic, artificial,

---

[19] Suzanne Gordon, *Prisoners of Men's Dreams: Striking Out for a New Feminine Future* (Boston/Toronto/London: Brown, Little, 1991) ch. 1.

[20] Gordon, *Prisoners of Men's Dreams*, 4.

and overly abstract ... but if cultural products articulate too closely with the specific social environment in which they are produced, they are likely to be thought of as ... parochial, time bound, and fail to attract a wider and more lasting audience. The process of articulation is thus characterized by a delicate balance between the products of culture and the social environment in which they are produced.[21]

The Gospel of Luke is itself a study in the problem of articulation and its author provides important coordinates for how the subsequent community of faith might similarly engage its cultural setting. Luke's narrative theology shows the degree to which (1) the message of Jesus might be communicated in the language and cultural conventions of one's world, (2) how one can engage in this communicative task while at the same time participating in discourse that specifically challenges the status quo, and (3) the dangers of simply blending into the dominant culture are constant.

Like the women's movement about which Suzanne Gordon is concerned, the disciples in Luke are presented as ever in need of being warned of too simply adopting the values and practices of the respected. Beware of the Pharisees! They practice hypocrisy, substituting their own concerns for holiness and honor for God's concerns with care for society's little people (12:1). Beware of the scribes, for they have made a life out of behaving like people who are outside of God's family, spending their time trying to win respect and to be treated as benefactors (20:45–47; 22:24–27). These warnings are not theoretical, for the disciples in Luke show their own proclivities to such behavior.

That Luke's presentation of the story of salvation engages with while subverting wider cultural institutions can be easily illustrated. Earlier, we saw how Luke embraced the cultural power of patron–client relations in order to subvert it; we made similar observations about the presentation of Jesus' table fellowship. A third example derives from the Evangelist's presentation of Mary in Luke 1, the contours of which stand in

---

[21] Wuthnow, *Communities of Discourse*, 3.

stark contrast to the introductions of other characters in this chapter.[22]

In introducing Zechariah and Elizabeth in 1:5–6, Luke devoted considerable attention to issues of status. He draws immediate attention to their socio-religious status, their purity, and their righteousness. They are children of Aaron, who share in the advanced, hereditary honor of the priesthood (cf. Exod. 28:1; 29:9; Numbers 18). Zechariah has kept his priestly status above any possible reproach by his marriage to a "daughter of Aaron." What is more, by means of scriptural echoes our introduction to Elizabeth and Zechariah invites our association of them with Abraham and Sarah (cf., e.g., Gen. 11:30; 15:16; 16:1; 17:1, 17; 18:11–12). Further, they are old (1:7) – and that in a society where honor comes with age. Clearly, Luke is a person of the honor/shame-oriented culture of the Mediterranean world. Even Joseph, whose script in the Third Gospel is extraordinarily passive, is presented to us as one with an enviable birthright (1:26).

What, then, of Mary? According to Luke, she is (1) a Galilean, distant from the center of Jewish holiness; and (2) a virgin betrothed to Joseph. She is thus characterized as young (10–13 years) and not yet sharing in the honor of Joseph – her betrothed, not yet her husband. Her family (one's immediate source of status) is not mentioned. Indeed, she is not introduced as in any way deserving of honor.[23] Indeed, her insignificance seems to be Luke's primary point in his introduction of her here, for this is immediately contrasted with Gabriel's declaration of Mary's favored status (1:28, 30). Within the world of Luke's Gospel, she holds a lofty place in God's eyes. Moreover, she claims membership in God's household (1:38). This is her family. That is, she derives her status from God, so that Luke here begins his presentation of a community of God's people whose fundamental social experience is grounded in their relationship to God.

---

[22] Joel B. Green, "The Social Status of Mary in Luke 1,5–2,52: A Plea for Methodological Integration," *Bib* 73 (1992) 457–71.

[23] That Mary is a "relative" of Elizabeth (1:36) does not in any way alter this image. Συγγενίς is sufficiently vague to imply nothing about Mary's participation in the priestly line for which Elizabeth is noted.

Thus, in his characterization of Mary, Luke has begun to undercut the conventional competitive maneuvering for positions of status prevalent in the first-century Mediterranean world. Mary, who seemed to measure low on any status scale – age, family heritage, gender, and so on – turns out to be the one favored by God and the one who finds her identity ultimately in her obedience to God and participation in his redemptive purpose.

To push the problem of articulation further, the reality that "cultural products" are shaped by their social situations should serve as a reminder that Luke's vision of the new world of the kingdom may be even more profound than he has narrated. For example, in spite of the ample material on women in his Gospel, Luke has come under criticism in recent years for largely leaving women in their expected roles in the patriarchal world of the first century. Luke portrays women as having accompanied Jesus from Galilee to Jerusalem (8:1–3; 23:49, 55); why not as exercising leadership in ways that break further out of expected norms? Why not a discipleship of equals? It has been suggested that Luke has thus closed the door on an earlier, more radical Jesus movement in which women were full leadership partners, unconstrained by any social mores.[24] Although such a thesis cannot be proven or disproved, we may wonder nevertheless how possible it would have been for such a picture of the early Christian movement to appear against the background of larger Greco-Roman society. Charges of compromising the liberating message of Jesus are always possible, of course, but one must also face the reality that that message was and is always articulated and incarnated in conversation with wider cultural forces. Do we expect too much of Luke (or tradents before him) when we question his attitude to and representation of women against the backdrop of our own, changing cultural background? Jesus and the early church, including the Third Evangelist, like those of other creative moments, faced the necessity of working

---

[24] Cf., e.g., Elisabeth Schüssler Fiorenza, *But She Said: Feminist Practices of Biblical Interpretation* (Boston, Massachusetts: Beacon, 1992) ch. 2.

within the constraints of one's historical particularity while at the same time calling (some of) those constraints into question. What may be of greater consequence for our appreciation and appropriation of Luke's message, then, is the way issues of status, including those related to gender and sex, have been condemned in the Third Gospel. Does this not open the way toward a discipleship of equals?[25]

CERTAINTY AND HISTORY

"Crucified under Pontius Pilate." This statement of the Apostles' Creed is one of historical certitude with which few today would take issue.[26] It is not the sort of statement in which Christians have typically been interested, however, and it is certainly not the sort of statement on which Luke focused. The cross is paramount for Luke, but he presents it not as historical fact but already in interpreted dress, as central to the divine purpose (e.g., 24:26–27). When accounting for Luke's claim to historiographical intent (1:1–4), we must not confuse his literary agenda with the motivations of a disinterested chronicler of events.

It is we, people of modernity, who cry out for historical certainty. It is we who want to know "what really happened": "just the facts." As a consequence, we have taken our yearning to Luke and, on occasion, found him wanting. His record of a census under Quirinius, instigated by Emperor Augustus for the whole world, is a prime example (2:1–7). The problems are legion,[27] but the least capable of explanation is its chronology: Jesus is understood to have been born during the reign of Herod the Great, but Quirinius did not serve as governor of Syria until some ten years later. The immediate question of

25 This expression, "discipleship of equals," is taken from Elisabeth Schüssler Fiorenza, *In Memory of Her: A Feminist Theological Reconstruction of Christian Origins* (New York: Crossroad, 1983).

26 See Joel B. Green, *The Death of Jesus: Tradition and Interpretation in the Passion Narrative*, WUNT 2:33 (Tübingen: J. C. B. Mohr [Paul Siebeck], 1988) 1–2.

27 See the summary in I. Howard Marshall, *The Gospel of Luke: A Commentary on the Greek Text*, NIGTC (Grand Rapids, Michigan: Wm. B. Eerdmans; Exeter: Paternoster, 1978) 99–104.

historical veracity aside, it is worth noting the implausibility that Luke would have made such a factual-sounding statement had he expected his readers immediately to question its accuracy. To put it another way, whether or not we are able to prove its factual nature, we may still understand that the statement was placed in the narrative purposely, "to identify the census with events which would have been familiar to the reader. Unlike the historian, the reader was unlikely to have been familiar enough with the dates of Quirinius's governorship to quarrel with the narrator's chronology."[28] Whatever else it does, the note about the census contributes to the historical realism of the account and situates the birth of Jesus in an interpretive context wherein the overlordship of the land of Israel by Rome is paramount.

Earlier, in chapter 1, we noted that Luke's historiographical aims were profoundly hermeneutical. He was interested in signification – not merely with "what actually happened" but especially with "what it means." Recent developments in the enterprise of history-writing have taken our understanding of this task in a direction more congenial to our comprehension of what Luke has accomplished. Thus, it is worth noting that since the 1960s the positivist distinction between "what actually happened" and "what was perceived to have taken place" has been clouded. Historians commit to writing what has already been interpreted by others together with their own perception of those interpreted events, and in so doing produce a text that is itself susceptible of interpretation. This text participates in and parades (one or more) interpretive agenda.

On the one hand, this brings to the foreground the reality long observed by ethnographers that antedating "official" records of a community's past by an (outside) historian is a series of community-determined choices of retrospection. Significance is already attributed to events by political decisions implicitly and explicitly made about what will be remembered and in what terms. On the other hand, we are now more aware

---

[28] Steve M. Sheeley, *Narrative Asides in Luke–Acts*, JSNTSS 72 (Sheffield: JSOT, 1992) 103.

that the writing of history is itself a relational event; "events" are already and always represented in their relation to the interpreter. To put it differently, the task of representation does not find its reference so much in "historical fact" as in perception. As a consequence, the utilization of narrativity in the representation of reality presents events within a structure of meaning.[29]

This does not mean that we must renegotiate our understanding of Luke as one who has been faithful to history. Rather, it requires that we reflect more accurately on how we all relate to history and, thus, understand Luke's achievement. And it requires that we reflect more fully on the sort of "certainty" Luke purports to provide his audience (1:1–4). As we have tried to show, the Gospel of Luke is not fundamentally interested in certifying that Jesus did such-and-such a thing. Rather, he worked to present Jesus' deeds within a web of interpretation. The Third Evangelist was representing reality as he understood it. In doing so, he shaped events to a teleological end, emphasizing their standing in the divine purpose. By this means, he sought to legitimate (his depiction of) "the events that have been fulfilled among us" together with the Christian community rooted in God's aim.[30]

This means, too, that we must reject any attempts to locate in Luke an historical basis for faith.[31] Luke's construal of "the events" is already "faith-full," for he has perceived and represented them already within a theological perspective by which he apprehends the world. His narrative is already proclamation, kerygmatic history, preaching with history.

Finally, if we learn from Luke that history is never grasped

---

29 Brian Stock, *Listening for the Text* (Baltimore: Johns Hopkins University Press, 1990) 108; Mary Douglas, *How Institutions Think* (Syracuse, New York: Syracuse University Press, 1986) chs. 6–7; Wolfgang Iser, *The Fictive and the Imaginary: Charting Literary Anthropology* (Baltimore/London: Johns Hopkins University Press, 1993); Clifford Geertz, *Works and Lives: The Anthropologist as Author* (Stanford, California: Stanford University Press, 1988).

30 Cf. Joel B. Green, "Internal Repetition in Luke–Acts: Contemporary Narratology and Lukan Historiography," in *History, Literature and Society in the Book of Acts*, ed. Ben Witherington III (Cambridge University Press, 1995).

31 *Contra* Hans Conzelmann, *Theology of St. Luke* (London: Faber and Faber, 1960).

neutrally, that events are always understood within an interpretive framework in relation to communities of interpretation,
perhaps we will also learn from him the importance of our
engaging today in reflective analysis of history-in-the-making.
By situating the story of Jesus firmly in the scriptural story of
Israel, Luke announces the transcendent significance of the
coming of Jesus. In fact, in this rendering, the story of Jesus is
now gathered into the story of God. This gives the events
surrounding the mission of Jesus new perspective, but it also
vouches for the continuing presence of God's redemptive
project. By continuing the narrative into Acts, Luke accomplishes an analogous task, showing the ongoing achievement of
God's aim, through Jesus, in the early church. Following Luke,
Christians today may reflect critically and constructively on
the degree to which the church persists along the trajectory of
God's salvific plan, witnessed in the Scriptures of Israel, clarified and executed in the life and ministry of Jesus, carried on in
the first decades of the Jesus movement. We may learn better to
grapple with the charge to explore how God is at work in the
world, to ascertain how God's saving activity in daily human
existence is continuing, to detect evidences small and great of
the in-breaking kingdom of God in the commonplace of everyday events, and to ensure that our life together is oriented
around serving God's work.

FAITH AND WEALTH

In his study *Sharing Possessions*, Luke Timothy Johnson astutely
observes, "Although Luke consistently speaks about possessions, he does not speak about possessions consistently."[32]
What is "the Christian approach to possessions"? Bringing this
question to Luke, we find no straightforward answer. Should
we completely renounce possessions, as Jesus counseled the rich
ruler to do (18:22)? Or is (restitution and) the giving of alms an
adequate response, as in the account of Jesus' encounter with

---

[32] Luke Timothy Johnson, *Sharing Possessions: Mandate and Symbol of Faith*, OBT
(Philadelphia: Fortress, 1981) 13.

Zacchaeus (19:1–10)? Luke's reticence to provide a code of behavior on this question is symptomatic of the complexity of the questions involved, but also of the Lukan mandate to struggle with finding context-appropriate ways to realize the summons to repent integral to the good news. For this struggle, Luke provides a number of coordinates.

First, faith and wealth belong to the same arena of life. Luke allows for no segregation of life into spiritual and secular, church and world. Recent study of religion and economic values in the US suggests the distance between Luke's message and that of many Americans. Although in theory most believe God cares what they do with money, this has apparently little effect on how that money is actually spent. Although almost three-quarters of the US labor force believe that greed is sin, only slightly more than one-tenth think it wrong to want a lot of money. More than three-quarters thought having a beautiful home, a new car, and other nice things is either "very important" or "fairly important."[33] For Luke, such separation of stated beliefs from routine practices is diabolical.

Attitudes and behavior around wealth never escape the scrutiny of the gospel. This is not because wealth is inherently bad, nor that poverty is inherently good. Rather, it is that both wealth and poverty can serve as or provide for obstacles to obedience to the divine mission. In Mary's Song, both the hungry and the well-fed need divine action in order that they might join hands as recipients and agents of God's promise (1:53).

"Wealth" is for Luke never simply "money" (or its equivalent in money-less societies); it is "Mammon" (16:13), an almost hypostatized power with respect to which one can never remain ambivalent, neutral, or passive. Wealth becomes a master if it is not mastered; it exerts itself over against the lordship of Yahweh and thus over against the qualities of care for and solidarity with the poor counseled by the Scriptures and by Jesus (16:10–15). It is not for nothing that John's

---

[33] "Does Faith Influence Spending?", *Christianity Today* (26 April 1993) 57: a report on Robert Wuthnow's project on Religion and Economic Values at Princeton University.

immediate response to those who inquire into the pattern of repentance demanded by the coming of the Lord is in each case related to wealth (3:10–14). Nor is it by chance that Luke carefully observes that discipleship entails "leaving everything" (e.g., 5:11, 28).

What is enigmatic is that this "leaving everything" cannot in every case be understood literally. Levi "leaves everything," then gives a great banquet for Jesus (5:28–29). In the early community in Jerusalem, people were able from time to time to sell property to provide for the needs of the church (Acts 4:34). Perhaps the best commentary Luke provides on "leaving everything" comes in Acts: "No one claimed private ownership of any possessions. Instead, they had everything in common" (4:32). Luke thus borrows from widespread conventions for sharing among friends in a community (e.g., Plato, *Republic* 449C; Aristotle, *Nicomachean Ethics* 1168B). He presents the question of possessions as less a question about wealth and more an issue of treating others as members of one's own extended family. To put it differently, discipleship for Luke requires that one not cling to possessions as their slave, but that one give precedence to others of God's household and especially to others in need.

Closely related is the counsel of Luke that followers of Jesus adopt the perspective of those in need. This Lukan message is presented in a subtle way by the nature of the narrative itself. Who are Luke's primary characters, the ones with whom Luke's auditors are invited to identify? To whom does the good news come? A barren couple, Zechariah and Elizabeth; Joseph and Mary, too poor to provide any sacrifice other than "a pair of turtledoves or two young pigeons"; shepherds watching their flocks by night; a widow whose only son has died; and so on. Moreover, in interpreting the Scriptures, Jesus repeatedly adopts the interpretive location of those in need; that is, he reads Scripture in a way that favors those in need (e.g., 4:16–30). Today, with the possibility of our living antiseptic lives removed from the nearby cries of the poor and when we are conditioned not to think of ourselves as poor, this must surely entail our working to find ways to give a voice to the voiceless and developing an ear for what has previously been tuned out.

In spite of our relative affluence, Robert Bellah and his associates have drawn attention to the poverty even of those of us who live in countries like the USA.

Yet the truth of our condition is our poverty. We are finally defenseless on this earth. Our material belongings have not brought us happiness. Our military defenses will not avert nuclear destruction. Nor is there any increase in productivity or any new weapons systems that will change the truth of our condition.[34]

Of course, to speak in such terms is already to bring to the fore a further, related aspect of Luke's message. Poverty and wealth are never alone as mere questions of economy. As we have seen, "the poor" may appear in many guises which would include those living at a level below what we today call "the poverty line," but not only such persons. Hence, what one does with one's own money is never the only question; wealth is imbued with wider social meaning and embedded in other cultural norms: "money is power." Like Zacchaeus, those of us living in relative affluence may be confronted with our deficiencies so as "to rejoin the human race, to accept our essential poverty as a gift, and to share our material wealth with those in need."[35]

THE LIFE OF THE SPIRIT

According to the Third Gospel, the coming of God's redemption into the world arrives by way of divine initiative, but God invites children, women, and men to employment as "helpers" in his program. The shape of Luke's narrative is such that characters within the story and readers and auditors who enter into it are all confronted with an invitation and choice. As we have observed, the Evangelist is involved in a communicative task; he narrates the story of Jesus so as to achieve certain ends – above all to assist his audience in the process of discerning, embracing, and serving God's salvific purpose. The "certainty" promised to Theophilus is the hermeneutical

---

[34] Bellah *et al.*, *Habits of the Heart*, 295–96.   [35] Bellah *et al.*, *Habits of the Heart*, 296.

grounding of the mission of Jesus and those who follow him in God's plan.

For communicating God's purpose, Luke recognizes the importance of the Scriptures, but gives particular eminence to the Holy Spirit. The eschatological Spirit has become active to reveal, but also to guide and to empower. Luke understands Jesus to operate throughout his ministry in the sphere of the Spirit's direction and power. And he understands that those who will continue Jesus' mission, the divine project, must also receive the Spirit and move forward under the Spirit's influence. This is one way of describing the major motif of Luke's second volume, the Acts of the Apostles. The indwelling presence of the Holy Spirit in the lives of Jesus' followers is anticipated in the Third Gospel; its realization and effect is narrated in Acts.

Life in the Spirit cannot be taken for granted, according to Luke. Jesus himself, God's Son, nurtures this life by his balance of prayer and public engagement. We repeatedly find him in a prayerful process of discerning God's will in order to persist along the path of divine service. For him prayer and fulfillment of his vocation are symbiotic – each leads to and cultivates the other. His disciples are instructed to pray, and it is noteworthy that, following Jesus' exaltation, we find them repeatedly (and continuously) in prayer (e.g., Acts 1:12–26). For them, too, serving the kingdom of God and prayer are balanced ingredients of life in the Spirit (e.g., Acts 4:23–31).

This is life before God and in God's service as envisioned by Luke. This vision treats as parts of the whole what has so often become segregated in the life of the church, not least in modern times. Which comes first, "the spiritual life" or "work in the world"? Would Luke even recognize the premise informing such a question? To take one example, followers of the Social Gospel and its children have often criticized others for being too heavenly minded to be of any earthly good. Christians of a more pietistic bent have scored points off those actively engaged in social witness, inquiring: these public displays of goodness – where do they come from? Do they grow out of a changed heart nurtured by prayer and worship? Luke's Gospel points an accusing finger at these dysfunctions. The Gospel of Luke may have as its program "bringing good news to the poor," but it is also the Gospel most interested in prayer and praise and spiritual retreat. The "spiritual life" envisioned by Luke is none other than that which led Jesus to identify with God as Father and Son, to retreat in prayer to God, to participate in exceptional discourse on scriptural interpretation already as a child, to win for God praise from the crowds, and to embrace a style of living in the world that could only lead to the Place of the Skull. Prayer and world-engaging life are woven into the same fabric of life in the Spirit.

Perhaps Luke sees no tension between these and other elements of Christian life because he views none of these alone as the aim of that life. In the end, Luke is concerned to highlight only one aim – the aim of God to bring salvation through the life, death, and exaltation of Jesus; salvation in all of its fullness; salvation to all peoples. For those who embrace this purpose, the empowering and guiding activity of the Holy Spirit is available, as is a new relationship with God as Father and with the community of God's people as extended family. What is needed is the decision to embrace without reservation God's work. What is needed is the reorientation of life around one purpose, the purpose of God.

Further reading

A number of bibliographies are available to assist the student of the Gospel of Luke. Among the more helpful are the following three:

Bovon, François. *Luke the Theologian: Thirty-Three Years of Research (1950–83)*. PTMS 12. Allison Park, Pennsylvania: Pickwick, 1987. Provides a series of thematic essays discussing Lukan scholarship from 1950 to 1983, with extensive bibliographies on history and eschatology, the use of the Old Testament, christology, the Holy Spirit, salvation, discipleship, and the church.

Green, Joel B., and Michael C. McKeever. *Luke–Acts and New Testament Historiography*. IBRB 8. Grand Rapids, Michigan: Baker, 1994. Lists and annotates some 500 titles, the vast majority in English, under such headings as Bibliographies, Surveys, and Histories of Research; Classic and Contemporary Approaches to Luke–Acts; The Genre, Unity, and Purpose of Luke–Acts; The Theology of Luke–Acts; and Issues in Lukan Historiography.

Van Segbroeck, Frans. *The Gospel of Luke: A Cumulative Bibliography (1973–1988)*. BETL 88. Leuven University Press, 1989. Lists almost 2,800 Lukan studies during the 15–year period ending in 1988, then provides thematic and verse-by-verse indices.

Other studies helpful for studying the theology of the Gospel of Luke include the following:

Cadbury, Henry J. *The Making of Luke–Acts*. 2nd ed. London, SPCK, 1958. A classic and comprehensive exploration of the literary process and rhetorical concerns leading to the production of Luke–Acts.

Conzelmann, Hans. *The Theology of St. Luke*. London: Faber & Faber, 1960. Much study of Lukan theology has taken its starting-point from this ground-breaking redaction-critical study. Although most of Conzelmann's conclusions are now disputed (e.g., the periodization of salvation history, Luke's "early catholicism," Luke's interest in and knowledge of Palestinian geography, etc.), this book nevertheless draws attention to key aspects of Lukan thought that deserve exploration.

Fitzmyer, Joseph A. *Luke the Theologian: Aspects of His Teaching.* New York/Mahwah: Paulist, 1989. Eight studies on Lukan themes extending the important synthetic treatment of Lukan theology found in Fitzmyer's commentary (see below). Topics include authorship, the infancy narrative, Mary, John the Baptist, discipleship, Satan and demons, the Jewish people and the Law, and the death of Jesus.

Gillman, John. *Possessions and the Life of Faith: A Reading of Luke–Acts.* ZSNT. Collegeville, Minnesota: Liturgical, 1991. A brief but wide-ranging summary of the Lukan perspective on faith and wealth that accounts for contemporary scholarly discussion.

Maddox, Robert. *The Purpose of Luke–Acts.* SNTW; Edinburgh: T. & T. Clark; FRLANT; Göttingen: Vandenhoeck & Ruprecht, 1982. Argues that Luke wrote to reassure an increasingly Gentile church of the validity of its faith in spite of Jewish rejection of Jesus and the gospel.

Marshall, I. Howard. *Luke: Historian and Theologian.* 2nd ed. Exeter: Paternoster; Grand Rapids, Michigan: Zondervan, 1989. An introduction to Luke's theology emphasizing Luke's value as a historian, his theological accord with his sources, and "salvation" as the key Lukan concept. The second edition contains an addendum surveying Lukan studies in the 1970s and 1980s.

Moxnes, Halvor. *The Economy of the Kingdom: Social Conflict and Economic Relations in Luke's Gospel.* OBT. Philadelphia: Fortress, 1988. Integrating cultural and anthropological studies with compositional and redaction-critical approaches to the Third Gospel, Moxnes portrays the social world of the Gospel of Luke in which the Evangelist's concerns with social and economic issues find their meaning.

Powell, Mark Allan. *What Are They Saying about Luke?* New York/Mahwah: Paulist, 1989. An excellent, panoramic introduction to the contemporary study of the Gospel of Luke.

Tyson, Joseph B., ed. *Luke–Acts and the Jewish People: Eight Critical Perspectives.* Minneapolis: Augsburg, 1988. A useful point of entry into current discussion on this central issue in contemporary study of Luke–Acts, with contributions from J. Jervell, D. L. Tiede, D. P. Moessner, J. T. Sanders, M. Salmon, R. C. Tannehill, M. J. Cook, and J. B. Tyson.

Among the many recent commentaries now available on the Third Gospel, the following are of particular importance:

Evans, C. F. *Saint Luke*. TPINTC. London: SCM; Philadelphia: Trinity, 1990. A pericope-by-pericope discussion of the Gospel, sometimes more theological in orientation, sometimes more historical and tradition-critical.

Fitzmyer, Joseph A. *The Gospel according to Luke: Introduction, Translation, and Notes*. 2 vols. AB 28–28A. Garden City, New York: Doubleday, 1981/85. A massive commentary from a tradition-critical approach, also providing a history of recent research on each pericope. A sketch of Lukan theology is included (1:143–270).

Johnson, Luke Timothy. *The Gospel of Luke*. SP 3. Collegeville, Minnesota: Liturgical, 1991. A helpful literary analysis of the Third Gospel, concerned with "what Luke is saying and how he goes about saying it" (xii).

Marshall, I. Howard. *The Gospel of Luke: A Commentary on the Greek Text*. NIGTC. Exeter: Paternoster; Grand Rapids, Michigan: Wm. B. Eerdmans, 1978. A commentary on the Greek text of Luke, emphasizing historical- and redaction-critical issues.

Nolland, John. *Luke*. 3 vols. WBC 35. Dallas, Texas: Word, 1989–93. A reading of the Greek text of the Third Gospel understood "as an exercise in communication, deliberately undertaken by the Gospel writer with at least some focused sense of the actual or potential needs of his audience" (xii).

Index of biblical texts

156

Index of modern authors

Index of subjects